GET REAL!

Fighting the Mythic Woman

Finding Your Authentic Self

Ananya S. Rajan

Copyright © Ananya Sri Ram Rajan 2010
www.mythicwoman.wordpress.com
mythicwoman@gmail.com

Published by Lulu.com
www.lulu.com

All rights reserved. No part of this book may be reproduced, stored in a retrieval system, or transmitted by any form or by any means, electronic, mechanical, photocopying, recording, or otherwise, without prior written permission of the author, except for brief quotations in critical reviews and articles.

ISBN 978-0-557-53077-9

To Balaji, Sahana, and Siddhartha:
May we always provide solace and strength to each other. I love you more than words can say.

To my sisters who keep me sane with love, laughter, and chocolate. The OWL awaits us.

Contents

The Myth Realized	1
The Power of Myth	8
The Mythic Woman	15
Identity or One's Essence	24
It Starts with a Little Girl	40
A Culture That No Longer Serves Us	58
The Myth of Keeping Silent	68
The Myth of the Ugly Duckling	74
The Myth of the Super Mom	78
The Myth of Power and Control	84
The Myth That You Aren't Complete	87
The Image and the Reality	90
Finding Your Sense of Self	95
Exercises 1-7	97
Creating a New Culture	115
My Story	121

Acknowledgements

As many authors have already stated, published works never happen without the help of a number of different people and institutions. So often our libraries are taken for granted and we don't realize how precious these institutions are until we don't have them. My sincere thanks to the staff at the Roosevelt University and Algonquin, Illinois libraries; you always made the lonely feat of writing and research much more interesting and successful.

A deep gratitude to the number of women with whom I have crossed paths whether it be for five minutes or what feels like a lifetime. The list is too long to mention all of you, but you know who you are. Many of the conversations we had, provided more insight into the issues women face fighting the Mythic Woman, so thank you!

To Michelle Barry, Beth Fisher, Deneene Florino, Ashwini Nelson, and Linda Taylor who read and provided critical feedback for my manuscript; without your support and encouragement this would not have happened; my loving appreciation to all of you.

To Elizabeth Valencia who read and reread many versions of this book and was exceptionally helpful despite her incredibly busy life. I cannot thank you enough for the thoughtful feedback you provided. Your life is an example of the strength that women have and often don't realize.

To Gomes who kept telling me to stop thinking and just write; such good advice from a fellow author.

To Subha for your affectionate present and marks of respect. I love you dearly.

And thank you to the one man who read my manuscript without judgment or jest. As always, your support and critical eye has made me a better individual and lady writer.

This I Believe

I believe everyone is born with an Authentic Self. I believe as young girls, women are not encouraged to be who they truly are. I believe this leads to women having a harder time discovering their own sense of Self. I believe this because there are more myths about women than men. I believe many of these myths do more harm to women than good. I believe that these myths shape the way women see themselves and the world around them.

I believe women have a harder time discovering their Authentic Self because they play many different roles in their lives. I believe these roles and how they are played are determined by society and a patriarchal pattern. I believe women today have accepted this determination and continue to play the roles assigned to them without thinking about how it is affecting their future or the future of their daughters. I believe this keeps the myths alive. I believe by keeping these myths alive, women will continue to lack self-determination.

I believe the Authentic Self is not about what others think of you, but what you think of yourself. I believe it is not about what you think will make you *feel* good, but about what *is* good for you. I believe that when we live from the Authentic Self we live not only for ourselves, but for others.

I believe women need to say what they mean, and mean what they say. I believe women hold the power of language. I believe the true language of women comes from the heart. I believe speaking from the heart is only possible when we know our Authentic Self.

I believe the Authentic Self lies within every person. I believe in order for women to find their Authentic Self, they need to understand the myths that have created their history, which governs their lives, and will influence their future. I believe women can change their lives by discovering who they are as individuals. I believe by changing their lives, they can change the world.

I believe that when women find their Authentic Self, they will discover how to live in balance. I believe that when women discover how to live in balance, they will teach the world to do the same. I believe this will begin the reconnection of humanity to Mother Earth. I believe this is our only hope for a future on this planet. I believe this is why this book was written.

The Myth Realized

When I started writing this book, I kept asking myself "how did all this start?" I was in the midst of a personal crisis that crept up on me faster than I realized. After seventeen years of raising my two kids and making the conscious choice to stay home with them from the time they were small, they were both leaving home. While I knew my daughter was ready to fly the coop at the age of twelve if we had let her, I was not ready for her brother, two years her junior, to do the same. But it happened that way. The year my daughter went off to college (having just turned seventeen), my son was accepted to an academy where he could pursue his love for theatre. While I had about six months to adjust to the change, it hit me like a brick wall one morning.

In my state of denial I kept saying it wasn't empty-nest syndrome and I would bounce back. My self-talk consisted of constantly reminding myself that I was resilient and strong, that I had been through worse, that my children were only a phone call away, and that their absence wasn't permanent. Like any major change in one's life, it made me question why I was going through it. Why was I having a hard time shifting back to being who I was before I had kids, before I became a mom, before roles took over my life?

As I thought about this, I began to think about women's lives in general. More often than not, a woman leaves the home of her parents as a daughter, goes to college or work, starts a home with a partner or friend, and eventually fills the role of partner, parent, or employee, then the role of a grandparent or elder. Granted, this doesn't happen to all women. But most women marry or commit, and have children whether biologically or through adoption. And often we do it automatically, like there is a program within us—which there is, if one looks at it from an evolutionary point of view. Our bodies are made to reproduce because of our instinct to survive.

On a deeper level, the change taking place in my life made me think about loss. The loss of what had been, the loss of my children as babies, the loss of my role as a "mommy," and then the loss of myself. Somewhere along the way, while playing the roles of wife and mother, I lost myself. I couldn't remember what my dreams were before I had kids, before my whole life was consumed with making sure the mind and spirit of my babies were nurtured. Who was I before these beings came along and swept me off my feet?

I didn't feel angry or upset, just disconnected. Disconnection can be powerful because everything becomes magnified. It's kind of like being in limbo. You are neither here nor there. Many people experience this when they have lost a loved one or have been through a traumatic experience. Suddenly everything seems loud, bright, or just too much to handle. The word "raw" is often used, almost like our nerves are on the outside of our skin instead of being safely tucked away. Because of the amplification, we see things in a different way. And that is what happened to me.

It was during this time that I was introduced to the work of Peter Senge. Peter leads an organization called the Society for Organizational Learning (SoL) and after my husband attended one of Peter's seminars, he came home with a couple of books to read and then a recommended reading list. Daniel Quinn's book *Ishmael* was on the list and caught my eye because it was previously recommended to me by another friend and happened to be sitting on our bookshelf. I am of the belief that things happen for a reason no matter how tragic they can be. The universe puts opportunities in our path. It is up to us to be aware of that opportunity and make the choice of whether or not to take what falls in our lap and do something with it. Needless to say, I began reading *Ishmael*.

Reading has always provided me comfort. I love being part of a character's life, listening to their thoughts and getting a different perspective. Sometimes it's a gift to let yourself drift away into someone else's life so you can forget your own. But that didn't happen with *Ishmael*. I came across a line that read "that is the myth you have been led to believe" and suddenly I saw my life and the lives of women in a whole new way.

I went from thinking about the loss of my identity to the loss of the identity of all women due to myth. I thought about the most well-known female archetype in the Judeo-Christian realm, Eve, and the bad rap she was given. I thought about how this led to women being taught to be ashamed of their bodies and how we were brought up to believe that we were "less than." And finally, I thought about the incredible damage that hundreds of years of this mentality has created for women, and still continues today.

I began to consider the expectations set upon women by society, and how they shape the way we think about ourselves. At first I thought my theory was out in left field, but the more books I read, the more I realized there was a bigger problem than my empty-nest syndrome. The expectations set up by society, while not written down anywhere, have led many women to lose who they are as individuals. I don't doubt my own situation led me to feel this way, but it was also prevalent in other women I talked to. While many were content with their lives raising kids, working to pay bills, and generally going along, something was missing in their lives that they couldn't figure out. I know this sounds familiar to what Betty Friedan termed the "feminine mystique," but I thought it could not possibly be the same problem considering how much had changed since she wrote her book.

The universe is a funny thing. If you put out a thought or intent, be prepared for the response. Books of all kinds that focused on the various emotional and psychological difficulties women faced in their lives began to come my way. One could say that I was looking for a problem and therefore found it, but it was more than that. Authors such as Mary Pipher, M.G. Lord, Judith Warner, and Wendy Shalit, were not writing off the tops of their heads. They had evidence to show something was and is wrong and unless we wake up to the question at hand, the cycle will continue. Interestingly, it was a letter from my mother that validated my feelings that something was amiss.

 In an effort to find myself, I thought I would go back to work. While looking for an old resume, I came across newspapers that I had kept from the time I was a young girl. In between the headlines that read "Nixon Resigns," "Ford Pardons Nixon," "John Lennon Dead at 40," was a neatly folded letter to my father written almost fifty years ago. In her beautiful handwriting, on onion skin paper, my mother poured her heart out to my dad asking him to forgive her. She stated that her behavior was due to her own jealousy of his life as a doctor and his freedom to socialize, while she was home taking care of kids and feeling very lonely and cut off from everything. She missed being a nurse and having her own identity. Ironically, my mother has been dead for thirty years, and here I was, fifty years later, going through a similar situation.

 When my daughter was about six, I had read Mary Pipher's best-seller *Reviving Ophelia* and thought "I won't have these problems with my daughter. I'll make sure she has a strong sense of who she is." It was an arrogant statement. All females, at some point in their lives, will question who they are and struggle with their identity. It is inevitable because of the physical, psychological, and emotional changes females go through. Our bodies make us very aware that we are no longer little girls, and if our bodies don't, our male peers will. Granted for some, the process will be easier than for others.

 In my state of mind, I thought about the struggle that all women have to find their Authentic Self. We are the only gender that has to make choices that have an intrinsic impact on our lives. Yet, many of the choices we make throughout our lives are influenced by the myths that have molded women's lives for centuries such as the stories we are told as little girls, the mythical messages from the media, and the ridiculous standards we strive to fulfill as grown women. For me personally, I began to recount the number of things I was told as a child about being a "good girl." Good girls didn't talk loudly, spoke only when spoken to, crossed their legs when sitting, kept their hands on their laps, and were always well-kept. How else would she get a husband? Men, according to the myth I was given, weren't attracted to strong, independent women.

While I sound like the ideal daughter of Miss Manners, a mental pattern was set in my psyche that limited my thoughts and kept me focused on the frivolous instead of on my intelligence. My mother, bless her heart, believed that I would get through life with my looks, find a guy, fall in love, get married, and that would be that. She believed this despite having strong leadership skills in high school, being the head of her sorority, graduating at the top of her class, and eventually becoming a nurse. (However, one of her goals as a nurse was to find a successful, dynamic doctor and marry him, which she did. She just didn't realize the impact that choice would make on her own sense of self.) For me, the indoctrination of being a "young lady" and a "good girl" left me confused and disempowered as I went through my teen years. Mentally molded to worry about my looks and being attractive to boys, I was left without knowing how to set boundaries of any kind because I was following a myth that was handed down to me from my mother and her generation.

Another factor that made my own adolescence difficult and chaotic was seeing other girls who didn't follow the same pattern or myth. My upbringing and the influence surrounding me was different from theirs. Boys and beauty were not their priority. They were interested in athletics, academics, and had a quiet confidence about them. I wanted to be like them, but they didn't fit the pattern of how I was told to be, so I didn't know how to adjust my pattern to fit theirs. The inability to stand up for myself from the bullies of the neighborhood or to decipher between someone befriending me because of me or for their own gain was difficult, if not painful. Such inabilities as a child often follow us right into adulthood. How many women do you know who cannot discriminate between a partner who truly loves and cares for them and one who just wants handouts?

My realization made me ask, "Who makes this stuff up? How did we get here? And why do we continue to follow these myths?" But most importantly, how do we change it? How do we stop allowing myth to determine our lives? The visceral realization was empowering, but frightening at the same time. It was empowering because I realized that we can create something better for ourselves as individuals and as women, but it was frightening because the possibilities were limitless. Like the female birth control commercial that asks, "Who says we have to have twelve periods a year?" I began asking, "Who says we can't change the way we think about ourselves and the expectations of society? Who says we have to follow the myths handed to us by society? Who says?"

These are the questions I explore in this book from a historical, cultural, social, and spiritual point of view. I look at the history of myth that has surrounded women, how it has been maintained through religion and philosophy, how these myths became reality through science and medicine, how these myths continue to dictate our lives through the media and advertising, and how women continue to perpetuate the myths by their actions, because the examples of anything different are few and far between.

But becoming aware of the Mythic Woman is only one part of the problem. In order to step out of the mythic mindset that dominates our lives and step into living an authentic life, we need to know how to get back into touch with our own identity and our Authentic Self. When we live authentically, we make decisions which not only benefit us, but do no harm to others. When we release ourselves from societal expectations, we begin to live a life of joy and mental freedom. We no longer stress ourselves out worrying about what others will say or think, but instead, we focus on what brings serenity and strength into our lives.

The Power of Myth

One of the most powerful stories we are taught as children is the creation myth because it answers the profound questions in our lives such as: Who are we? Where did we come from? Why are we here? Where do we go when we die? Like a compass that provides direction to those at sea, myth gives us structure and direction. Many of us who have a belief system tend to do so because of a creation myth that was told to us by our family or loved ones. It is the creation myth we are given that acts as a springboard for beliefs we hold later in life.

Myths are the stories created by dominant groups of people that set the tone for a culture. They are harmless until they are taken as the truth. When we think of a myth as the complete truth, we accept it as part and parcel of our reality. We no longer question its origin, or the impact it makes on our lives or the lives of others. In other words, we no longer ask questions such as, "Where did this belief come from?" or "Does this belief really work for me?"

To give an example, consider how powerful the Judeo-Christian creation myth of Adam and Eve has been on the lives of women in the Western world. While it is now considered "misinterpretation," women, once upon a time, were made to believe that the reason they menstruate is because Eve ate the apple. And today in some faiths, and by some people, it is still a belief. Imagine how women must feel to be reminded that they are descendants of a woman who was considered wicked because she had a mind of her own!

Later, qualities of dependence were emphasized in fairy tales. In order to live in happiness Snow White, Cinderella, Sleeping Beauty, and Rapunzel, all had to be saved by their princes. By repeatedly being introduced to such examples, women unconsciously feel they are not complete without someone (mainly a man), or that they need to be rescued or saved. They hesitate to make a decision on their own or express their thought, because all their life they are shown examples of women being rescued. Belief in such a myth can be stifling and determine the way we interact with the world. But that is the power of myth. It becomes an integral part of our lives, sometimes to our own detriment.

While many of us know the interpretation about poor Eve as a disobedient, unfaithful, and cunning woman, what many don't know is that the female was held in high regard as far back as 40,000 B.C., roughly 36,000 years before Eve was destined to suffer in childbirth. In what is now France, totems to represent the feminine principle were abundant. Study of Paleolithic burial sites created during these early times in history show totems, figurines, cave drawings, and pottery, honoring women because she was thought to hold the mystery of life and death. From the study of cave drawings, archaeologists believe our ancestors did not understand the connection between sex and reproduction. It was thought that women were solely responsible for the production of children. Therefore, the female or Goddess, and what she represented, was honored and worshipped like the male God or patriarchal figure is, today.

It may have taken time for our ancestors to figure out the correlation between sex and reproduction, but they didn't need any help understanding that the production of children ensured their survival. Interestingly enough, according to Riane Eisler in her book *The Chalice and the Blade*, it is believed that during the time of matriarchy, women lived in equality with men and that power "was more equated with responsibility and love than with oppression, privilege, and fear." Given how positive the images of women seemed then, I often wonder what it would have been like to be raised under such influence.

Like anything in life, change was inevitable. Unlike the Goddess-worshipping societies of old that revered the earth, fertility, abundance, and the important roles *both* sexes played, the Proto-Indo-Europeans male worshipping societies, whom Marija Gimbutas traced back to originating from Russia, slowly wore away these practices and cultures over thousands of years. With the change in power, came the change in myth. Thus we have, as Merlin Stone relates in her book *When God Was a Woman*, the snake as the symbol of wisdom, fertility, sacrifice, and a woman's connection to nature during the Minoan period in Crete, ancient Greece, and other cultures, transformed into the serpent who whispered to Eve to eat the apple. Sexual union once considered sacred because it produced life, became sacrilegious and perfunctory. The natural processes of a woman's body such as puberty and menstruation, events still celebrated in some cultures and considered a rite of passage, were proclaimed as dirty and a form of punishment from God. And women's intuition and connection to nature were considered as blasphemous and evil.

As these are all part of a woman's life, it is no wonder that we have groups of women, such as the goddess movement, that work towards changing the dominant view of sex and the changes the female body goes through. It is interesting to note that, in general, there are more books about intimacy and sex for women than for men, more books about dealing with puberty, periods, and adolescence for girls than for boys, and more books for women to help them reconnect with their intuitive nature. We often never question why this might be so, or even consider the fact that women write about these things in order to uncover an innate culture that once belonged to the female. Once, long ago, the female was honored. Menstruation was not only a time of change, but a time of power. The fact that sexual union with a woman produced life was considered awe-inspiring. And women, at one time, knew this because it was part of their culture. It is difficult to believe that women then felt the insecurities they feel now, because at that time the culture recognized the power they held and honored them.

When I mentioned the idea for this book to friends of mine, the thought of being dubbed the "weaker sex" ran through my mind. How did women go from being honored to being known as the weaker sex? In reality, female babies worldwide have a lower mortality rate than male ones. When I casually approached women with this thought, they would pipe up and say, "Yeah, I've always wondered where that idea came from!" If I mentioned it to men, they seemed too scared even to touch the topic with a ten-foot pole. However, my friend, Pablo, who has a PhD in microbiology and studies metaphysics, gave me another way of looking at it. He cautiously clarified that he didn't view women as the weaker sex, but from a physical standpoint he said he could see how it could be interpreted as such.

Like much of what I had read about the origin of the myth of the weaker sex, Pablo talked about energy. Many ancient traditions (and now various fields of science) study the thought that there are two forces in nature, the active and the passive. With the craze on *feng shui*, almost everybody is familiar with the yin/yang sign, the sign of polarity. It is a circle divided with black on one side and white on the other. Within each color is a small dot of the opposite color. The two sides represent the energies of nature. The circle represents everything in its totality, the black represents the female (yin), and the male (yang) is white. Female energy is considered passive, dark, mysterious, developmental, cold, and moist. The male energy is considered active, light, open, accessible, hot, and dry. Neither force is greater than the other, nor can one exist without the other. Each gives the other purpose, or a reason for existing and a way to know itself. According to Chinese medicine, we carry both energies within us and to have too much of one puts the body out of balance and makes us feel unwell.

Pablo's point was that these forces manifest themselves in nature right down to the creation of life. It is the egg that lies immobile in the recesses of a woman's body, while it is the sperm that moves and is active. When a woman is pregnant, the pregnancy causes her, toward the end, to be more stationary due to the weight and her own internal instincts to "nest." And as babies rely on their mothers for food, it is the woman who nurtures her young (considered passive, I guess), while the men are free from such ties. Pablo also mentioned the way women and men differ in their own ways of being: women are considered inward, thoughtful, they work through emotions and feelings, while men are considered outward, say what they think, and work through things mentally. I am deliberately using the word "considered" because this way of being does not apply to all women or all men. It is a *perceived* norm based on the characteristics being observed in a majority of people.

Pablo also discussed the scientific point of view in Western thought. In Western science, the belief that "everything is one" is something rather new. The concept of unity in diversity is an underlying thought in Eastern mysticism. However, quantum physics has opened new doors to old thinking in a language that makes it accessible for everyone, those of the rational logical mind and those of the philosophical, esoteric mind. Pablo stated that science looked at things from the greater-than-less-than point of view. With the rational logical mind that focused only on materialism, effectiveness, and the economics of things, the "weaker," "passive," "subtle," or "unseen" just wasn't considered good enough. It was the stronger, more powerful, "in your face," more rational force that made the difference.

This comment reminded me of something I had once read about Aristotle (384-322 B.C.). Viewed as one of the greatest thinkers, Aristotle's thoughts were considered scientific in his time. Today as we look back at a few of his thoughts, some women find themselves angered by the contribution he made to their subjugation. Aristotle had no doubt in believing women were inferior to men. He premised that heat caused the development of the body and as women were smaller than men, their bodies did not produce enough heat. He also theorized that women did not produce enough heat because they carried more fat and were rounder than men. Based on the fact that women's bodies were smaller, he assumed their brains were smaller too. So women, according to Aristotle, could not possibly be as smart as men and hence needed to be governed. Women, according to Aristotle, were "naturally deficient."

Historically, male thinkers of various kinds continued to build from such thought, all from the perspective that women were infantile in thinking, needed to be governed by a man, were too feeble-minded to have an education or work, or were physically incapable of much else than producing children and tending to home and hearth. Using the mythic female figures, whether from the Bible or from modern day TV, we recognize traits that we feel are acceptable and unacceptable based on how they are portrayed and received. Thus we associate the "good" woman with the Madonna and the "bad" woman with Mary Magdalene—to use an old example from the Bible. Bringing this example up to date, think of the number of TV shows where there is one female who is considered the "bitch," or how the media sets one female Hollywood star against another. One of the more recent diva rivals set up by the media was between Lady Gaga and Christina Aquilera. The two women seem to have admiration for one another, but the media doesn't make money on niceties so a rivalry has to ensue. It wasn't until Aquilera personally commented on her website about her admiration for Lady Gaga's courage that an end was brought to the controversy.

This latest hullabaloo is a perfect example of the myth that women, who are powerful and talented, are catty and can't get along. By continually viewing women in such light, the myths about women are kept alive. By reinforcing the image that women are infantile and desperate for attention or that if they are successful they are "bitchy," makes women strive to be better. We strive to be different. We want to be liked, to be the good girl, the good woman. So we work harder and worry more about what "others" will say, because we don't want to be "that woman." Think about the number of times you've said yes to an event you didn't want to attend. Or hosted a holiday dinner when the world is crashing down around you and you can't really handle one more thing. Ever wonder why we have books about *Women Who Love Too Much*? Or *Women Who Do Too Much*? In our effort to be better, we strive to be the archetype of the perfect woman, or as I call her, the Mythic Woman.

The Mythic Woman

In the early 1980s, soon after arriving in India, I was fortunate to spend time in the presence of the spiritual teacher, J. Krishnamurti. "Krishnaji," as he was known to some, spent his whole life studying the Self and the human condition. He is famously known for telling his followers that "Truth is a pathless land," and constantly asking his audience "Who are you?" and "Why are you here?" While his questions were not unusual for a spiritual leader to ask, his method of addressing those questions was unique, because he did not provide a direct answer. As he spoke, Krishnaji would address how our mind works. He would talk about how we look to others for answers, an authority of some kind to tell us what to do. And he would include himself in this category and say, "Don't listen to the speaker. Think for yourself."

To this day, I am eternally grateful for the experience of crossing paths with Krishnaji. His writings often clarify issues for me and have encouraged me to observe my thoughts. Likewise, others who visited with Krishnaji often found his peeling back of the layers very insightful. However, there were also those who viewed him like a guru and pleaded with him to fix things in their lives. Krishnaji recorded many of these visits in his writings and they can be found in his popular series called *Commentaries on Living*.

One theme that Krishnamurti returns to again and again is suffering, because it is so prevalent in our lives. Interestingly, many women who visited with Krishnaji would talk about the anguish they were experiencing because of the loss of a partner, child, or even a parent. Aside from the physical loss of the person they loved, the emotional turmoil these women felt was often due to the identification they had with being a wife, mother, or daughter. The *role* they played defined who they were. Without it, they did not know where they stood in the world. Their life revolved around being the person others wanted them to be based on the roles they played. In other words, they existed for others; they did not *live* for themselves.

There is a huge difference between existing and living. When we live, truly live, we feel a kind of magic in our lives. Things begin to fall into place and everything feels right with the world. We begin to connect the dots in our life and are able to see how our actions lead to the events which take place around us. When that happens, we realize that we are the ones who control our lives. The process is very powerful and there is often a sense of freedom that reigns over us. Unfortunately for most of us, these periods of peace and clarity come in spurts. It does not happen all the time. It does happen, however, when we are answering our heart's desire and doing something that we have longed to do; or when we direct our lives through the choices we make for ourselves. In other words, we don't allow others to make decisions about our lives for us.

Existing is a different story. While I am sure we have all felt that we exist for others and are not really living, existing is more than going through a period of monotony. Existing is when we give others control of our lives, whether it be the people who surround us or the messages we receive from the media. We don't make choices based on our own inner promptings, but follow what others tell us. We wonder why we can't find happiness in our life, but in reality, we aren't living our lives based on our own decisions, but on what others want us to do. When we exist for others, we lose touch with our inner self and, in turn, become mythic women who live according to standards dictated by society, our friends, or even our work. We realize something is missing in our lives, but we don't know how to step out of the pattern we are following.

And just what is it about the standards set by society that make us follow them? Standards provide what we think is the ideal and the Mythic Woman strives for the ideal. She is the perfect woman many women strive to be. We may not strive to be perfect in *all* areas of our life, but choose an *aspect* of our life. So there are women who spend their days exercising to have the perfect body, or women who play the "good girl" and don't confront anyone or speak their mind; or women who constantly feel they need to take care of everyone while putting their own needs last. The Mythic Woman focuses on being perfect whether it is physically, emotionally, or mentally. And this isn't to say we shouldn't have standards in our life, but the standards the Mythic Woman lives by are the standards set by others.

Interestingly, I don't ever see men having to contend with perfection, but somehow women, old and young, have felt they need to compete with the concept. From the time we are little girls, there is something instilled in us that makes us believe we have to be better. The constant attention to this ideal (that does not exist) keeps us from truly living our lives. When we strive for something outside ourselves, we lose touch with who we truly are. We exist.

Unfortunately, the culture that surrounds women has always been based on standards. First it was set by men, religion, and the patriarchal society, then by professionals like doctors and "authoritative" organizations, and today it is set by the media. And the standard keeps on changing, so we keep changing to keep up with it. Yet, when we make those changes, we often don't realize that we're not making choices of our own. We do it because we are told repeatedly what is best for us through our upbringing, television, and talk shows. If the movie stars are doing it, we do it too, because (at one time) they seemed to have all the answers.

To give an amusing example of this, the movie *Simone* comes to mind. In this film, Al Pacino plays a director who gets fed up with the demands of his female stars and creates a computerized actress. Simone (Sim One) becomes an overnight sensation. She is the ideal female movie star. She is beautiful, soft-spoken, has the perfect body, and is talented. She is easy to work with, shows up on time to work, and doesn't have a lot of demands. What makes her even more attractive is that she is inaccessible. Because she isn't real (which, of course, no one knows), Pacino's character promotes her as a reluctant starlet who loves what she does, but is wary of the press and her popularity, and this makes her more enticing to people. For her audience, Simone's uniqueness stirs something within them that they can't put their finger on; and though they don't even know her personally, there is a relationship between her, the admired, and her fans who admire her. She is the myth that cannot be attained, so is desired even more. Her fans want to know her and she becomes their obsession. When Pacino's character eventually confesses that Simone is nothing but a computer simulation, no one believes him. Simone is too real to everyone. She is part of their lives. Like Simone, the Mythic Woman doesn't exist, but she is very real in our lives.

As a culture we like to believe in myths and sometimes we will accept the image over the reality. Lady Diana Spencer was a shy nineteen-year-old preschool teacher who flourished into Princess Diana after her marriage to Prince Charles. While it is difficult to ever really know how Diana felt about the constant attention she received, the media created a larger than life image of her when, in reality, she was just another person.

From the time Diana was brought into the media's eye, she was scrutinized and deemed as the perfect princess. Nothing about her was kept private. Her supposed virginity was talked about when she married, her incredible shyness was translated as being demure so she didn't look socially awkward, and when she produced to two male heirs, she cemented her perfection by ensuring the future of the Monarchy. After Diana's divorce, she bounced back from heartbreak and took up causes considered uncommon among the British royals, thus creating a relationship between herself and the everyday person. But in the beginning, she was marketed as the ideal—the Mythic Woman—and to contend with that culminated in Diana suffering from various disorders. However, the upheavals forced her to find her authenticity and break away from the expectations that everyone else had of her. She found no fulfillment in being what everyone wanted her to be.

At some point in her life, every female has lived the life of the Mythic Woman. Only a woman knows the Mythic Woman because she battles with her every day until she comes to a point in her life when she decides to step out of the pattern and be her own person. Nowadays, this is slowly happening, but the influences that keep the Mythic Woman alive are more powerful and more subtle than a woman's own free will. Every woman is reminded of the Mythic Woman because, at the one extreme, she is the latest reality star on the cover of a magazine or the model that promotes a make-up "to make you look years younger;" and at the other, she is the mom who rigidly follows the advice of the latest child psychologist, or the woman who follows the diet that will take pounds off in a week, and so on. It is this and more that creates and keeps up the Mythic Woman's appearance.

The Mythic Woman is old, but she never ages. She is constantly metamorphosing into a younger and younger version in every generation. She is handed down from one generation to the next through the myths and messages given to us by our mothers and the women who mold us. She was once created through creation myths and fairy tales, but she now takes form in the TV shows we watch or the advertisements that blare at us. While at one time the Mythic Woman was told that she needed to please her partner by looking attractive and behaving in a certain way to get his attention, today's Mythic Woman acts like it doesn't matter and that she is liberated. But as mentioned before, the Mythic Woman doesn't make her own decisions, because the decisions have already been made for her. And it isn't until we desperately try to step out of the pattern, that we realize how rigid it is—and how subtle.

It amazes me how small the distinction is between the stores my daughter shops at for clothes versus the ones I visit. There is little difference. It drives me nuts that manufacturers feel women in their forties can wear the same jeans as a twenty-year-old. And while some forty-year-olds can, I can't. Yet, I often find my shirts and blouses at the clothing stores my daughter visits. But this is an example of how the Mythic Woman is maintained. By giving fewer choices to women about what they can wear, we are forced to dress in the same clothes our daughters wear, thus continuing the "hip and youthfulness" for which our culture is so well-known.

I went shopping for jeans soon after turning forty-three and could not find a pair of jeans that fit comfortably. Mind you I don't wear designer jeans. I wear blue jeans bought at the local Farm and Fleet. I like real blue jeans. To be on the safe side, I wore the same pair of jeans that I had bought just a year earlier at the same store. While I knew my body had changed, I could not believe it had changed so much that I could no longer fit into the same size. What had changed was the size and cut of the jeans. Jeans manufacturers like Levis and Lee no longer make jeans for women whose bodies are aging and rounding with time. They design jeans so you HAVE to be the shape you were when you were twenty. I remember becoming despondent and going home.

In reality, it had nothing to do with me—yes, I am heavier than I was in my thirties, yes I have changed my diet, yes I do exercise—but I'd rather wear skirts for the rest of my life than cram my body into a pair of jeans in order to say I wear a size six, which, in reality, is cut for a person who is a size two! But in order to wear what manufacturers make, women will diet and exercise their lives away; not realizing it isn't about them. It's about industries promoting and maintaining an image in our culture. And one could argue that this is all in my imagination, but walk into any sports store and try buying a pair of sweatpants. Once upon a time, sweatpants were to work out in, now they are to show one's athletic body. I'm still trying to figure out how exercise apparel became part of the fashion industry.

The Mythic Woman is maintained in other ways as well. She represents the "good girl," the woman who won't speak up because she doesn't want to cause a fuss, or the woman who works in corporate and doesn't talk about being a mom when on a business trip, because she doesn't want to appear "domestic" and incapable of being away from home. She is the woman who feels a man probably knows better or is smarter than she is. Or even the woman who feels she is just not doing enough or not doing something well enough. Most of us would say that we don't intentionally feel this way or behave this way, meaning we don't feel this way *consciously*, but even women who hold powerful positions "feel out of place and inauthentic in traditionally masculine organizational settings," according to Alice Eagly and Linda Carly in their book, *Through the Labyrinth: the Truth about How Women Become Leaders*.

This may be because women often have to choose. When starting a family, it is often the woman who needs to choose whether to put her career on hold in order take care of her children. While many women do this willingly, the point is that women are the ones who have to choose, because they are the ones who physically must deal with childbearing and all that comes with it. And should circumstances warrant one of the parents to stay home, it is often the woman, not the man, who does so; not because she is expected to, but because she usually makes less money than her husband. Interestingly, the economic downturn of the past three years has put more women back in the workforce than men, as many of the men out of work held middle management positions. Despite this, women continue to earn much less and are employed in positions needing either little skill or part-time hours.

But choice, especially life choices, can often keep us from feeling authentic about our decisions, and therefore mythic. I remember trying to work a full-time job in part-time hours while taking care of my children. Like many parents, I didn't get home until after my kids were home from school and I went through the whole conundrum of whether they were too young to be home alone even though it was only for a few hours. I reiterated to them not to tell anyone they were home alone, to make sure the doors were locked, to not answer the phone unless it was me or their father, and then I would fret like crazy if I didn't get a phone call once they were home from school. Eventually, I realized I didn't feel authentic at my job or authentic as a mom. It didn't seem fair to me that I somehow could not completely let go and focus on my job, like my husband did, despite being a mother. And while I was home, I was thinking about work.

The mythic side of us quietly puts up with this. If we didn't, there would be more attention given to women in the workforce to accommodate our changing lifestyles. When I discussed this with an overworked mother, she rolled her eyes and said, "Well, what are you going to do? We can't change everything." In reality, the circumstances many women find themselves in as working mothers often make them too tired and preoccupied to even think about such ideas. And in a way, this continues the Mythic Woman lifestyle because we need to do what we need to do. Focusing on oneself, one's desires, or even how one can change the system is out of the question. Instead of living, we exist and wonder, "Is this all there is?"

As women and as individuals, we need to think about what we want in our lives and not as a wife/partner, mother/step-mother, sister, daughter/granddaughter, boss/employee and so on, but just as a person without any title, without any role, without anyone to make the decision for us, without any expectations. By responding to what we want from our lives, we come into touch with a deeper part of ourselves, our Authentic Self. Once we do that, we become aware of how much the Mythic Woman influences our life and we are able to turn her off. We stop living according to what others say and begin to follow our own inner path.

Identity or One's Essence

Have you ever had the experience of looking at yourself in the mirror and wondering who the person is looking back at you? It's like we wake up one day and realize we were so busy with life that we lost ourselves along the way. We wonder who is it exactly who lives our life. Is it authentically you? Or are you being the person everyone expects you to be? We are often many things to different people based on the relationship we have with them. But does this define the essence of who we are?

The concept of identity as it relates to one's inner Self or essence has been a topic of study in various fields of the social sciences. Psychologists tell us that we have many different selves, because we play so many different roles in our lives. But psychology looks at the Self as a concept; something we need for "mental well-being." This is true, but it is much more. The concept of the Self I would like to focus on is what the Buddhists call "beingness." Beingness is who you are without all the roles and the expectations of those roles attached. It is who you are when there is nothing to compare yourself to, no standard to live by. It is who you are *naturally*, if that makes sense. It is your own inner Self. Throughout the book I have deliberately capitalized the word "self" to emphasize that it is this Self that we need to answer to at the end of the day.

It is difficult to write about the inner Self or one's beingness. No one but you will know when you are in touch with it. No one can tell you what it actually feels like. There are no words that will describe it accurately because it is an experience and everyone's experience is different. For some, the experience is sacred. It is something that is very personal and profound, often difficult to talk about. For others, they will say that everything in their world *feels* right. Sometimes we feel completely in touch with who we are and at other times, we feel we are at sea with ourselves. I have met very few people who consistently feel they are in touch with their inner Self, because it is a process of great discipline and awareness.

Finding one's inner Self is like learning to ride a bicycle. It starts out being difficult, but after time and practice, it feels a bit more natural. It is not something that happens one day where you wake up and shout from the mountaintop, "Hey I found my inner Self!" (Well, I take that back, I did say everyone's experience is different. But I would question those who wake up and do so.) It takes practice because in today's world, we have moved so far away from who we truly are. And as women, we all have remnants from a long history of subtle (and not so subtle) psychological oppression. We struggle with the voices in our heads telling us we aren't good enough. In our minds we are never perfect the way we are. We are never acceptable. We constantly think we need to be better.

In the several discussions I have had with women, the question of where these thoughts come from and why we think this way have often surfaced. But the answer is right in front of us. The reflection of humanity is seen through our media. Television holds nothing sacred any longer. Personal problems that were kept behind closed doors and within a family are now blasted through the airwaves. Most of these problems center on women. Delicate topics like a child's paternity are made a mockery of on daytime TV shows. Young girls and women who starve themselves to be thin, parade themselves in front of a camera and cry on cue to have their five minutes of fame. Reality TV allows us to peer into the dysfunction of the rich and (in) famous. Shows such as *What Not to Wear* allow show hosts to belittle and make fun of those who dress for comfort and don't follow the fashion standards. (And granted, some people do need a lesson on daily dressing.) But sadly it seems to be women, more than men, who allow themselves to be made a spectacle of in the strangest ways. These are just small examples to show that while we can cry victim to exploitation, we contribute to our own victimization. And this, despite women throughout history, and even in today's world, being labeled as property; being beaten, tortured, and raped as slaves; kept from an education, and persecuted for being outspoken.

In her book *Finding Herself: Pathways to Identity Development in Women*, Ruthellen Josselson defines identity as "the stable, consistent, and reliable sense of who one is and what one stands for in the world. It integrates one's meaning to oneself and one's meaning to others; it provides a match between what one regards as central to oneself and how one is viewed by significant others in one's life."

Josselson states that in today's world, the formation of a woman's identity is one of the most important developmental tasks she can undertake. Our identity provides the foundation of who we are and how we make choices, or major decisions, in our life. Identity, like the girders that form the structure of a building, provides the structure to who we are as an individual. Once we have this structure, we can usually make healthy choices about how to fill out the rest of the building. This would include things such as our friends, lovers, hobbies, and what makes us who we are. But until we are able to establish our own identity, these things are difficult to choose because we have set no solid ground, no foundation.

The interesting point about Josselson's book is that it was published in 1990. Twenty years later, women are still trying to figure out who they are and what they want from life. We have plenty of people throwing ideas our way; and we have watched the effects of what women have gone through to try to keep up with the images and standards that have been provided by the media and society at large. The more that is thrown our way, the higher the standards rise; the more women compete to keep up, the more anxiety they have; the more anti-depressants they take, the more it is said that women "just can't seem to get it together."

From a cultural point of view, women have always had a hard time trying to find their sense of Self. I would have to say that many women *think* they know who they are based on the roles they play in their life. Becoming a partner, a wife, a lover, often gives us a sense of belonging or a sense of purpose. But a sense of belonging to another cannot provide an inner identity. One's inner Self doesn't rely on who one spends their time with, what one does for a living, or the clothes one wears. That doesn't explain who you truly are. The inner Self is a constant. It is influenced by the experiences a person goes through, but the genuineness of a woman does not come from whether she lives according to societal standards. Women have had a hard time with this. It is constantly expected that we should have a partner and be involved with a family, whether it is our own or taking care of our aging parents. And we are considered an anomaly if we don't follow this pattern. And most of us do, even when it is harming us emotionally, psychically, physically, or spiritually. We make the mistake of believing that the roles we play and the relationships we hold, define who we are.

After reconnecting with classmates from high school, it was interesting to see how many classmates, male and female were in unhappy marriages, how many were getting divorced, how many were divorced, and then how some of the women chose not to marry at all. So many of the women I talked to said something was missing in their lives. Could it possibly be that what was missing was their connection to their Authentic Self or their own identity?

Throughout time we have tried to draw attention to the need for women to have an identity in history. Most feminists know the story of Abigail Adams who sent a letter to her husband to "remember the ladies" when he was writing up the code of laws months before the independence of the United States. Abigail reminded him not to put "unlimited power into the hands of the husbands," and diplomatically stated that women will not be held by any laws where they had no voice or representation. Adams, unfortunately, did not listen to his wife so almost seventy-five years later women in long black dresses stood outside of the White House protesting for the right to vote. And who can forget Sojourner Truth's speech in 1851 to the women's convention reminding them "Ain't I a Woman?" Her speech showed women that identity, and the right to be recognized and respected, is not bound by ethnic background, language, religion, or even how much money one makes or doesn't make. Our identity and authenticity is what makes us unique and we all have a right to it.

Female writers from different races, periods of time, and walks of life have provided us their experiences, points of view, or even fictional examples of a different way of life in order to help us find our inner strengths and identity. Charlotte Perkins Gilman (1860-1932) introduced us to her controversial story *The Yellow Wallpaper* about a woman coping with post-partum depression and the constraints she finds herself under while being treated by her physician-husband. Gilman's work, for the number of years she wrote, was about women's self-determination and many of her stories are about women finding their inner voice and taking guidance from it. In Gilman's *Herland* written in 1915, she describes through the narration of a man and his two companions, a land that is occupied only by women. The women are self-assured, confident, lack any kind of fear, but are not dominating. They are kind but discerning and therefore cannot be taken advantage of. This non-patriarchal community of women has a connection with and a respect for nature, so they promote conservation, a concept foreign to their male visitors. Despite the story being politically radical at the time, Gilman gives us a glimpse into another way of being without completely turning our world upside down.

Black female writers like Toni Morrison, Alice Walker, Iyanla Vanzant, and bell hooks not only bring to light the horrors of slavery from a first person point of view, but show the emotional struggles Black women encounter even today. Their work also shows how sharing one's personal story can provide healing and resiliency for oneself and those who hear it. Resiliency and the ability to become whole again is something that lies within every woman, no matter what the color of her skin.

Latina writers and activists have also brought attention to the struggle to find themselves through their poetry, songs, and films. One of my favorite writers is Gloria Anzaldúa, who wrote from the Chicana experience, but whose words resonate deep within me despite the difference in background. The beauty of our inner Self is that it crosses the lines of difference set up by society. It is unique, because it is multifaceted; but because it is multifaceted, it can resonate with women from various walks of life.

Through their powerful words women can help remind one another what it means to be a woman and be human; as well as provide the tools needed to help us find who we are. This is why it is important for women to know and create their own history. By putting together writings, poetry, diaries, recorded recollections, even family recipes, we can get a glimpse into the *real* lives, the authentic lives, of our foremothers. While this isn't the "scientific" or orthodox way of putting together the history of a population, it is the only way to put together a history which relates to women because it is *about* women and their lives.

Unfortunately, there is so much about women's lives in history that we will never know because women either didn't have the education or the time to write it. The identity of women that we do get from history is that we were/are property, that we are nameless, and that we aren't as smart at math or engineering, and so on. These messages and myths have had their own consequences on our psyche. We have fallen into the trap of allowing the messages from what Carl Jung termed the "collective unconscious" to affect our lives.

Jung theorized that "in addition to our immediate consciousness . . . there exists a second psychic system of a collective, universal, and impersonal nature which is identical in all individuals. This collective unconscious does not develop individually but is inherited. . ." I believe that the constant messages and images to women telling us we are not good enough or "worthy" enough, that we are too fat or too skinny, too loud or too soft, make up the collective unconscious that as females we have all inherited. Such an inheritance is difficult to fight when trying to find our identity because it has become a second skin; most of the time we are unaware it is even there.

Today more women than men suffer from a lack of self-esteem which manifests into eating disorders, alcoholism, depression, and so on. It is prevalent even in girls as young as seven who now worry whether they will get fat. How can we focus on knowing ourselves when we have to fight the images and messages from something that does not serve us? Why do we *focus* on such images and messages when they do not benefit us? Think of the number of girls who as cheerleaders and athletes starve themselves to stay thin so they don't lose their place on the team. Some of these girls are as young as nine years old! Is it mentally and physically healthy for prepubescent girls to start worrying about their weight?

As psychologists have said, a lack of knowing who we are can be very detrimental to our well-being. We see it so often in child movie stars who suddenly don't know what to do with themselves once their role is over and they are no longer "cute." We see it in our girlfriends who are "boyfriend-holics" and can't seem to be without a man in their life. We see it in the young girls and women who count calories to stay thin or spend hours at the gym. Or even in our women friends who fret over making sure they throw the best party with the best décor and food. We put our identity into the superficial, wonder why we cannot find happiness, and then look for answers. We read books and the latest articles in magazines, talk to our girlfriends, try to follow the advice of talk show hosts, and think that others can give us the answers to finding happiness. In reality the only way to find true happiness is by finding our Authentic Self.

Women have always been at a disadvantage when it comes to finding their inner essence or "beingness" because we compete with outside sources that set an image of who and how we should be. For many years, hundreds to say the least, we have lacked self-determination, the ability to make decisions about our own lives and how to live that life, often not seeing the opportunities that come our way. Self-determination seems easy enough until one tries to put such ideas into action. We not only have to compete with the stereotypes against our sex and race, but we have to deal with the social expectations that create an image of how we are supposed to be.

For example, a friend of mine, who chose not to marry or have children, confessed that she was tired of being judged because she didn't follow the pattern. She related that because she wasn't tied to anyone, was over forty, and had been around the block a few times, she felt she had the freedom to be with whom she pleased. However, she said she felt judged by her own friends because she chose to sleep with men but not maintain any kind of committed relationship. "It's not like I don't know what I am doing. I don't get it. We talk about sexual freedom and the right to control over our bodies, but we judge the women who make the choice and act on it. Even in my forties I am made to feel like a slut by my peers. Why is it okay for men, but not for women?"

One reason may be the mixed signals we receive from the media which has been used to demonstrate to young girls what empowerment means, when in actuality the behavior promoted isn't empowering at all. It is empowering for the media and the advertisers who make lots of money selling the superficial to their audience. Young girls, in particular, are victims of this. Constantly wanting to be accepted and liked, girls will often move outside their comfort zone to get attention. The social expectations finally beat them down to being almost apathetic about their behavior. How can anyone know who they are when images inundate young girls from all angles?

An intelligent young girl told me once, with tears running down her face, how she would never get a boyfriend. This girl was beautiful, *but* she was also independent, knew what she wanted in life, and had a good sense of herself. She was the exception, not the rule. She refused to play the game of acting like she was stupid. "That's why boys don't like me. If I act stupid they think I'll let them take advantage of me." Despite the strength and intelligence of this young girl, the desire to "fit in" with the standards society was pushing at her began to whittle away her self-confidence.

Mary Pipher, in her book *Reviving Ophelia*, writes that "girls have long been trained to be feminine at considerable cost to their humanity. They have long been evaluated on the basis of appearance and caught in the myriad double binds: achieve, but not too much; be polite, but be yourself; be feminine and adult, be aware of our cultural heritage, but don't comment on the sexism . . ." This statement shows some of the ambiguity that many females face in our society today. But going along with the double standards or ignoring them will only worsen the crisis that many young girls and women find themselves in. It's been almost fifty years since Betty Friedan first spoke about identity in her book *The Feminine Mystique*. She called it, "The problem that has no name." While the book and its topic resonated with many women of that time; the media tainted what the women's movement was about by focusing on the bra burning issue and not on a woman's search for her identity and voice. At the time, the women's movement was a vehicle for women to campaign for equal pay for equal work and other issues prevalent to today's women. But as the focus was on the bra burning incident, radical feminists, and women being portrayed as "non-nurturing women," the public was sent mixed messages about the women's movement, which still has an effect thirty years later. It is no wonder that the minute a woman mentions the word "feminist" or "women's rights," our daughters and various women roll their eyes and hesitate to find out what it's about or don't want the word associated with them. And for women who do follow through and step out of the pattern set for us, it tends to be a source of contention.

In a cross-generational dialogue on the website of the "Evangelical and Ecumenical Women's Caucus," (**www.eewc.com**) two Christian feminists—seventy-two-year-old Letha and twenty-seven-year-old Kimberly discuss their views about what *The Feminine Mystique* meant to them. It isn't surprising to see Kimberly say, "I was surprised when I picked up Friedan and started feeling an odd resistance before I even read the first word of her book. I didn't know why I felt that way ... As Friedan herself says in an afterword to the book, it's the sensational, bra-burning, man-hating, anti-motherhood kind of feminists that the media has so often liked to give attention to. My good friend Jeremy once said to me, 'I have heard so much about that radical man-hating angry feminist. I just have yet to meet her.' I think he is right: she doesn't exist nearly as much as she is talked about."

Barriers like this stereotype are what women have had to constantly fight against. Such images of the angry woman, who is completely against any of the nurturing qualities so readily recognized and expected in most women, was one way to manipulate the focus off the real issue of women's rights—equality and identity. As long as women continue to aimlessly wrestle with the context of identity and their search for self, they will be unable to fight for the one inherent right of all human beings on this planet—equality. However, it is up to women to make this a reality. Too often women become the victims of their own doing. For years we have doubted ourselves and our own judgment, constantly believing that "someone else" knows better, knows more. In reality this has just caused our gender a number of setbacks.

Elisabeth Perle McKenna, in her book *When Work Doesn't Work Anymore*, writes that for years women have had to always "focus on what our superiors thought of us," but when we eventually find our own inner strengths, "we start to see, we too, are powerful." However, McKenna continues, "the largest obstacle to this perspective had been this reliance on outside forces and institutions to affirm and define us. As long as that dependence existed, we didn't take credit for our hard work. Thus, when our lives didn't turn out as expected, we blamed ourselves, not the institutions and the value systems that kept them propped up."

While McKenna's book discusses women who no longer find work as a way to define their identity, identity in itself does not rely on the affirmation of others, but on the affirmation of one's own inner promptings. The psychoanalyst Erik H. Erikson, in his book *Identity: Youth and Crisis*, first published in 1968, mentions that for women "it seems to be amazingly hard . . . to say clearly what they feel most deeply, and to find the right words for what to them is most acute and actual, without saying too much or too little and without saying it with defiance or apology." This problem still exists among women and young girls. We seem to lack knowledge of ourselves as full-fledged human beings, we depend upon the roles we play to define our Self, and we struggle to achieve the ability to verbalize the inner need we feel, without it subscribing to societal norms, without it being suggested to us by an outside force.

Such outside forces are not difficult to find in today's society. Since the women's movement of the 1970s, women as a population have not come to an agreement of what empowerment means to them. We can say that empowerment means different things to different women, depending upon their walk of life, and this is true; but what has happened is we have once again given up our own *inner* definition of what power means and have based the definition on how it is defined by the masculine principle. Therefore we see women in the corporate world dressed in a "power suit" (just like men), black pants and a white shirt with a black jacket, almost becoming "de-feminized." A friend of mine who works in Information Technology was once told to "tone down" her nail polish. She had gone on vacation and, before going back to work, forgot to take off the festive pink color she had applied for her cruise. Such color was seen as a "distraction" and her boss was afraid she would not be taken seriously wearing pink-colored nail polish.

At the same time, there are situations of women wearing office and daily attire that they feel "empowers them" because it emphasizes their female anatomy. And there are groups of women and young girls who feel that taunting these parts of their body to others is what makes them powerful and gives them a sense of identity because *they* feel empowered. They like the ability to "strut their stuff." Does emphasizing the anatomical parts that define our gender empower us and give us an identity as women? Is it really that simple?

Ariel Levy, authoress of *Female Chauvinist Pigs: Women and the Rise of the Raunch Culture,* brought to light the mixed emotions and hypocrisy of women involved in the show *Girls Gone Wild* (GGW). Levy provided dispatches for Slate.com about the show when she accompanied the crew while they collected material in Miami Beach, Florida. The compiled dispatches became part of her book. In one incident Levy describes girls stripping for GGW hats and T-shirts. In another incident, when a girl asks for a photo with the crew, the tour manager, Mia Leist, yells, "We don't want pictures, we want tits!" Ironically, Mia is a woman who blatantly admits she would never participate in any of the activities she asks other women to do. She says, "It's a business," and insinuates that it would be different if the girls were *not* volunteering to do it. And in still another incident, three girls are asked to make out with one another for the camera. When the shoot is over and the camera turned off, one girl confesses she only did it because the other girls pushed her into it. Demoralization quickly sets in and the girl finally says, "I hate Miami." So often we see such scenarios of women going against their own inner grain of what feels right to them, and the consequences of it.

When we do not live in tune with our inner sense of being, we live a life of division. We say things we don't mean, do things we don't want to do, and find ourselves frustrated, questioning our lives. Our desire as women to fit in with the majority (as crazy as it might be) is more prevalent than that of men. Most men don't have a problem setting boundaries and saying "no." It's almost like a "manly" trait. But women tend to be more social than men. We fret if we make a decision that doesn't follow the mainstream, we worry about being liked by others, and we often acquiesce to people's requests when we have no desire to, and we begin to feel resentful that we aren't stronger about our convictions. All of this has a major impact on our mind, body, and spirit, because we are not living authentically.

Not knowing our inner Self is similar to not knowing what we stand for. We have no foundation to start from that we can truly call our own. Psychology says that people, in general, base their self-worth on what others think. Women are known to do this. Some say it is biological, but I believe that most of it is cultural. Whether we are aware of it or not, we follow the given standard and worry about what others think. When we don't follow the norm, it is by "conscious" choice and we willingly deal with the repercussions that it entails because we are aware of the choice we make. What is most frustrating for women is the difference in standards. When a man sticks to what he believes in, he is considered strong in his convictions. When a woman is strong in her convictions, she is considered hard, outspoken, or called a bitch. To combat that perception, when we say what we believe in or stick to our own decision, we will defend ourselves and say, "I'm not trying to be a bitch but . . ." or we will defend our opinion to death. Why do we need to defend our right to make a decision or apologize for having a thought, opinion, or belief of our own?

We need to stop looking for permission to live authentically. It's not a women's right, but a human right given to every individual. It is interesting to note how much is written about women and their struggle to be heard, seen, read, and identified as individuals on this planet. As women, we think and behave differently from men because we are different. And for most women we struggle with owning our difference and accepting the difference in our own gender. Perhaps if we change our mindset from worrying about being a woman and the collective unconscious that goes with it, to being an individual who happens to be a woman, we may not only be able to change the way we view ourselves but change the societal mindset. (It's a thought.)

When we begin to live an authentic life, we "walk our talk." Our actions follow our words. We live from the heart. When we live from the heart, we find our center, our essence, our beingness. And once that is found, we have essentially found our true identity. We don't worry about what others say or do because we live from a place of equanimity. This equanimity is an important place to get to because we are so far out of balance. We need to stop making decisions based on what others want us to do and choose to do what we are capable of doing because we *want* to. We need to stop thinking we can do it all because of the Superwoman concept, happily delivered to us by societal standards of the good woman. Helping each other is a sign of strength, not weakness. It is time to get together with others and work for the same endeavor, aiding each other in our search for Self. While some may look at this as a spiritual quest, it is more important to look at this from a human rights issue. Not just for the women in this country, but for all women.

Finding one's sense of Self can only lead to the betterment of one's life and one's environment. I not only believe this, I know this to be true. I have seen it in myself, in my life, and in the lives of other women who choose to live authentically. And granted, once the decision is made, the work never ends. It becomes a commitment we make to ourselves as individuals born on this planet. It means living consciously every day, being aware of the choices one makes, and living from the heart.

One of the most powerful statements ever made to me was from a friend who told me that we come into this world with one life to live. That life is a journey filled with many roads and we have to choose what road we are going to take. We can change roads if we want, but it is up to us to decide. No one else can choose what is best for us. Likewise, no one but you can live your life. The journey can only be taken by the person it is given to. When we hand the reins over to someone else to make the choices in our life or allow them to run our life, we are not honoring the gift we have been given of taking our journey. The journey is a learning experience and an individual cannot learn if *he* or *she* does not make the choices needed in their life. To find out if you are living authentically, ask yourself *what* it is you are deciding, *who* made that choice, and *how* did you come to your decision. Of course the journey of one's life takes on a different aspect when you share it with another individual. We often believe we need to give up our aspirations and dreams when we commit ourselves to another, instead of viewing the relationship as an opportunity to learn from one another. But that's for another book.

It Starts with a Little Girl

I remember returning home from my doctor's appointment that confirmed my first pregnancy and hearing voices singing, "It's a girl, It's a girl, It's a girl." I tell everyone the angels were celebrating as I can't explain the event logically. But from that day on, I knew I was having a girl. Being a female who was raised to be the *über* female and all it entails, I decided I would make sure my daughter was raised differently. I did not want her to think because she was a girl she had to be different from being a boy. Mind you, I took the same stance when my son was born and to this day, I do not regret it. Yes, I am sure people wondered what my son was doing wearing nail polish to school or why he dressed like a girl for Halloween and passed it off very realistically. Or why my daughter was not interested in being the mommy while playing house, but left the boys to cook while she went to work. Somehow her self-confidence at the age of four was taken as being a bit of a bully because she was forthcoming about what role she wanted to play, and what she wanted to do when playing house. Her assertiveness did not fit the category of how a girl is "supposed" to be and I was very grateful for that, despite the complications it caused with other children who felt that she should "do girly stuff, not boy stuff." (And yes, my son was considered "soft" by some of the boys, because he wasn't as aggressive as they were.)

At the time of this writing, my daughter is in her third year of college and she admits that while going through puberty, she hated not being more of a "girly girl," but realizes that it benefitted her in the end. She is much stronger as a person than many of her female friends who vacillate in their decisions, worry about their bodies and whether boys find them attractive, and so on. My daughter says these aren't distractions for her and she doesn't allow them to be. She does have more male than female friends and while it might bother the girlfriends of her male friends, my daughter has no compunctions about keeping the record straight of what role she plays in the lives of her male friends.

I write all of this to show there is another way of raising our daughters. More so, that we *need* to raise our daughters differently if we are going to change the mindset and myths that have followed women from time immemorial. Women will often say they want to raise their daughters to be strong women, able to stand up for themselves, but the messages we give and the actions we perform are often worlds apart. If we are going to set a standard for our daughters to be independent, to have the courage to voice their opinions, to stand up for their right to be looked at as thinking individuals and not just bodies to be objectified, then we need to create an environment to make this happen. This is often easier said than done.

The concept of youth has always fascinated humans. Artists of all kinds have dealt with the different facets of youth through music, song, poetry, paintings, writings, and so on. And human nature, being what it is, we often struggle with the changes that take place right before our eyes when we look into a mirror. The reflection we see is often not what we feel inside. I remember when I was about seven or eight years old, I reached for a piece of fruit and realized my thumb was longer than I remembered it being. It was a funny realization to look at my hand and become aware that my whole body was growing. As children, we are fascinated with getting older and growing up; as aging adults we wish for backs that don't ache and legs that move a little faster. But while our bodies as children grow, it takes a little longer (and for some of us, perhaps even longer) for our minds to catch up with our bodies. The maturity of the mind and body do not happen in unity. (Perhaps that is why we have all heard our elders say "act your age," never really understanding *how we are supposed to act* for that particular age.)

Having been born in 1965, I can't say I have not been influenced by remnants of that time. In fact I don't really know any adult in this country, or even abroad, who doesn't look back at the 1960s as a time of dimensional change. It was the time when the concept of youth took over. An attractive young John F. Kennedy was President, there was talk of love and peace in contrast to the war in Vietnam, the Beatles made their British Invasion, the influence of Eastern thought made its way West, and there was on the whole a shift in thinking. Populations of people voiced the need for civil rights and risked their lives for it. Fear was thought of as something to be conquered and people took back their right to live without it. It was a momentous time.

In early 2009, I was lucky enough to see the revival of *Hair* on Broadway. The show and its cast were spectacular. One scene that caught my attention was when the character Berger is more interested in partying than in protesting the war and it leads to an argument between him and his love interest whose priority is being politically involved. Berger represents the population of people of the 1960s that never wanted to face the reality of what was happening. I thought to myself, "Yeah, I guess that was the drawback from that time," in reference to those who wanted to stay young and wild forever. As I later thought about it, the culture we live in today, where youth is glorified because it means we are modern and open-minded, is a thread from that time. But being open-minded can only go so far. We can raise our children with an open mind, but in the end, we are parents. We have the responsibility of setting a solid foundation, creating boundaries, and of being a protector and advocate for our children. Eventually, after they are older (and hopefully wiser), we can step back and play the role of guardian which allows them to make their own decisions, learn from their mistakes, and become better people because of it.

As parents we fight unseen forces and influences in our children's lives. One prevalent concern among parents is that advertisers and the media are taking advantage of our youth. In an effort to promote youth in our culture, more money in advertising and media is directed toward teens than ever before. Like teenagers who push the limits and boundaries to test their parents, advertisers and the media have crossed the line with their influence. Teens today are looked at as purchasing decision-makers because of the power they hold over their parents. Advertisers found their niche in the 1960s and have stuck to it ever since. The ever so slow changes that created more independence economically and socially for the women of the 1940s prompted advertisers to no longer just focus on the "happy housewife" (who persuaded her husband to purchase items), but on the young girls of the 1960s who would eventually become the "happy housewife." It is easy to see the transformation that took place in the minds of advertisers, for example, by looking at the history of the magazine, *Seventeen*.

In her book *Death of the Grown Up*, Diane West writes that the magazine *Seventeen* was originally started by a grandmother named Helen Valentine in 1944. It was the first magazine of its kind to focus on adolescent girls. The vision of the magazine was to "give stature to the teenage years, give teen-agers a sense of identity, of purpose, of belonging." On *Seventeen's* seventeenth birthday in 1961, editors wrote that the world in which the magazine was conceived was one where "teen-agers were the forgotten, the ignored generation. In stores, teen-agers shopped for clothes in adults' or children's departments, settling for fashions too old or too young . . . They suffered the hundred pains and uncertainties of adolescence in silence. . . ." Suffering the "hundred pains and uncertainties of adolescence in silence" is not something that will ever change. Adolescence is a difficult time for normal healthy kids, so one can imagine the stress it creates when the environment is chaotic and unsettled because of mixed messages from the media.

Unfortunately, *Seventeen* strayed away from its original vision. Today, like many of the other magazines for teenage girls, *Seventeen* seems to contribute to the insecurities that adolescent girls already feel with its focus on topics like sex, sex appeal, boys, how to please them, STDs, pregnancy, and so on. The "sense of purpose" it provides to teenage girls is that they need to please teenage boys and in order to do that they must look, act, and talk a certain way. Helen Valentine would probably not even recognize her own magazine if she saw it today. Instead of empowering young women, it discusses issues that distract a young girl from her own sense of self and identity. And this is not just dangerous for girls in their late teens entering womanhood, but for the "tweens," as they are called now, who are privy to *Seventeen* and its mature issues. Remember the thread from the 1960s and our desire to stay open-minded and hip? Today, we no longer have an unspoken demarcation line that keeps our little girls little and innocent, and our older girls, as role models of the responsible, independent, empowered young woman. That is now considered outdated and conservative.

In Mary Pipher's book *Reviving Ophelia*, the chapter called "Then and Now" describes a time when children were kept children. Pipher is almost twenty years older than I, but was raised during a time when sex, pregnancy, problems in another family, and so on, were not topics talked about in front of children. She recollects how two girls got pregnant and "disappeared" from her school and it was not until later that the girls of Pipher's age knew what happened to them. Hearing such a recollection brought back memories of a similar incident in my own neighborhood. The phrase "getting into trouble" meant one thing to an innocent six-year-old and another to the mothers who mentioned a teenage girl on our block getting into trouble. We were kept in the dark about such things, thankfully, so we could focus on more important things like how to throw a great tea party or play with our Barbie dolls!

But we've come a long way since then. Today, instead of Barbie dolls, we have Bratz dolls that teach our three-year-olds how to look "hot"; we have "kinderprom" to celebrate our five-year-olds "graduating" into first grade. And like prom, which juniors and seniors in high school attend to traditionally mark the end of their school years and the introduction and "promenade" into adulthood, five-year-old boys are expected to find a date, rent a tuxedo, and escort their date to "kinderprom." But why roll our eyes at that when we have TLC ("The *Learning* Channel"—what are we teaching and what are we learning?) introducing us to the reality show, *Tots and Tiaras*, where parents vicariously live through their toddlers by entering them into beauty pageants. Some of the children shown are too young to even talk, but parents babble on about how they will "need to sit down with their child and analyze what went wrong" during a performance.

Watching a clip of *Tots and Tiaras* reminded me of a spoof of a Mike Meyer movie starring "Mini Me." Parents stand with exaggerated facial expressions and gestures in an aisle near the stage playing out the whole routine their child performs on stage. One father of a two-year-old claimed he was the "king of pageantry" and was almost in tears when they didn't win anything. It was clear who wanted to win. Once done with her routine, the toddler was more interested in eating a cookie and playing with her brother than listening to her father who kept spouting off things for his daughter to do, as though she was a puppet.

The mothers who are interviewed for the show say it is what their children want, even when the child is screaming and crying while being sprayed with a tanning solution. Pageantry for tots is no different from pageantry for adults. Toddlers are introduced to fake teeth and nails, skimpy outfits which are supposed to look "sexy," sexual dance movements—that we were shocked and amused to see in *Little Miss Sunshine* (because it was a *movie*)—and bossy, caustic tongues that are unbecoming in toddlers and will be unrelenting when the girls become teenagers. But the parents, instead of parenting, give in to the child's every whim, even when the three-year-old is telling the adult to "keep quiet."

On the website of TLC, a subsidiary of the Discovery Channel, a small blurb introduces the show saying that it focuses on girls and boys, but it is obvious that the fashion and beauty industry for tots is centered on girls and this is what alarms me. Before a little girl is even old enough to talk, we are allowing them to be turned into sexualized divas. I specifically use the term "we" because as women, we are all responsible. We can say we don't agree with such shows and that reality TV has gone too far, but unless women voice their disagreement, no one will ever know. We can think that by not watching such shows, it is a quiet protest, and in some ways it is. But it will not stop TV producers from airing such shows or creating them. It is only when there are a number of protests, heard from a number of different sources, that a difference will be made.

M. Gigi Durham's book *The Lolita Effect* draws attention to the concern that women (and men) need to have about the exploitation of our young girls. It is interesting to note that she coined the term "the Lolita Effect" to describe the "mainstream corporate media construct of sex and sexuality in ways that actually limit and hamper girls' healthy sexual development." I believe that this unhealthy development of the "Lolita Effect" leads these young girls to become perfect models of the "Mythic Woman." The constant attention given to the body, one's looks, behavior, and so on, in order to be a sexual being, leads these young girls to focus on the materialistic and their looks, rather than their inner growth as an individual. They will grow to be women who will continue to follow the pattern of believing they are not good enough because they cannot keep up with the standards set before them.

The Lolita Effect shows that advertisers are targeting younger and younger audiences. There is no longer a sense of age appropriateness. While there is a concern today about how quickly girls are maturing and how teenagers participate in adult behavior without the maturity to cope with the consequences, as a society we don't seem to be aware that we've become victims of businesses that focus on the profits they can make by "empowering" young people with mythic messages. Females are more vulnerable to this than males because of the history and insecurities that females have had to combat for years. There are no ethics involved when it comes to making a buck, so the onus is on parents and guardians as to whether their children are exposed to things and at what age that happens.

Media, in itself, is a wonderful idea. The world has become smaller because of the Internet and cable television which allows us to view other cultures, see media from another country, and learn about the world in general. However, in the US, because of the First Amendment (for which I am all in favor), it is difficult to regulate the media and our exposure to it. And given our culture, which believes in the freedom of others, we are hesitant to impose restrictions, not wanting to look out of touch or infringe on the rights of Americans. This mindset has created a battlefield with some parents for and others against whatever the case may be. The media is allowed to create whatever it wants and as parents we have to fight to draw the boundaries of what we as guardians want our children to see and be exposed to. I know the difficulties of this because I have had my share of battles. And with media of all kinds being everywhere, how can we constantly control the influx?

When raising young girls, however, I think we need to be vigilant because the risks are so much greater. The myths that surround women are difficult enough for our teenage girls to understand and work through; what will the implications be for seven-year-olds who are worried about getting fat or how big their breasts will be? It is almost as though the whole thing is a sick joke on females. When does the female ever get a break from allowing herself to be objectified or from being objectified by our patriarchal society and the media? And the most difficult part of all of this is there is no agreement of what is appropriate and what isn't. Part of the problem of our "youth" culture is ambiguity.

  I am sure many parents have found themselves telling their daughters that their shorts are too short, their pants are too low and their make-up is too much. Yes, some of this is self-expression (while as parents we think they are just pushing our buttons). And not to defend the daughters who wangle their parents into buying into the sexualized version of adolescence, but what are girls supposed to wear when clothing manufacturers only provide clothing that parents find distasteful and inappropriate?

  One summer my daughter and I went shopping to find some outfits for her. Every pair of shorts my daughter tried on was just too short. My daughter follows in her father's footsteps. She is tall and slim and she has long legs. This particular summer she suddenly went from being a skinny kid to a shapely teenager, and while I think her legs are beautiful, I didn't feel it was appropriate for her to wear shorts that just covered her bottom and left so much of her legs exposed. She spent the summer wearing Capri pants because nothing we found was suitable. My daughter was not pleased with the situation, but I would not give in. Ironically, while we were in the dressing room of probably the fifth store we visited, I overheard another mother tell her daughter, "These are too short. You don't need your backside hanging out." I smiled to myself knowing I had company.

Sadly, for females we live in a world of hypocrisy and ambiguity. The media tells girls as young as nine to "flaunt it if they've got it" because it is empowering and they should be proud of their bodies. But change the channel and one can see Anderson Cooper doing an exposé on child prostitution in Thailand that shows a nine-year-old child prostituting herself out to a man old enough to be her grandfather. Sometimes that man is from this country. We don't understand how this can be happening to young girls, and yet, we don't see the connection between the nine-year-olds in Thailand and the nine-year-olds in our own country. Either way, it is the sexual exploitation of children.

And while much of the onus lies on parents to be more involved with their children, the media and its messages don't have to deal with the aftermath a tween or teenage girl goes through when she experiments sexually. The media doesn't have to provide guidelines to her about how to say "no" when she's just said "yes" to a boy who isn't going to stop. And it doesn't have to deal with providing strength to the girl who decides to keep her virginity until she's married, if such a concept exists any longer. The one thing the media does know how to do is set double standards, make reality shows, and make money. So we have teenage girls and young women baring their breasts and experimenting sexually with different partners, but being called a "whore"; or young women who are waiting until they marry to have sex and being called "prude" or "frigid." Either way she can't win.

Yet, a boy who has a reputation for being a "man whore" is looked upon as virile and a catch. And for some strange reason, girls don't mind having him as a boyfriend because he has a reputation and that notoriety will only move her up on the social ladder. Girls also believe that such a boy will only be with her. But boys are wary of girls who "have been around" and make jokes about "catching something." It is all a game, but one where the female remains subjugated to the whims and fancies of society, the media, and her own poor decision-making because of the pressure to fit in and the ambiguity of the messages she is given.

Simone Beauvoir, author of *The Second Sex*, was correct when she wrote "a woman is not born, but, rather, is made." Looking at toddlers on television who are told to "shake it," or "work it" shows that populations of parents are either completely unaware of the implications of what they are doing or they don't find anything wrong with it. We blur the lines between what is suitable for a female adult and a female child and place extraordinary psychological and physiological burdens on our young girls. Teenage girls are at a huge risk, being much more prone to depression than boys due the psychological impact of the biological changes on their bodies at puberty. And once the impression is made on a child, there is no turning back. Behaviors and attitudes we teach little ones are very hard to overturn when they become adolescents with minds of their own. So the impact put on a female child as a toddler will indeed have its effects later on in that child's life.

A study carried out by Dr. Denise Hallfors and her colleagues, published in the *American Journal of Preventive Medicine* in October 2005, found that the widely held notion that teenagers self-medicate and partake in sexual experimentation because they are depressed, may not necessarily be true. In fact, the study claims it may just be the opposite. Depression sets in *because* kids partake in these behaviors. Girls suffer from depression due to participating in sexual behavior and drug use, while boys suffer depression due more to drug use and binge drinking than sexual behavior. The study included over 13,000 youths from grades 7 to 11 and found that girls who participated in sexual activity were three times more likely to suffer from depression. In fact depression among teenage girls is being considered "the new STD" because it is so prevalent and has such a major impact on our female population.

    Depression among female teenagers isn't something new, it is true. There has always been the brooding teenager, but it is becoming more common nowadays and a concern that is catching the attention of social scientists. Timothy Strauman, professor and chair of the Psychology and Neuroscience Department at Duke University, collaborated with students on a study of why girls brood more than boys. The study was published in the journal *Development and Psychopathology* in 2006. "Brooding," according to Strauman, "is taking negative feedback and blowing it up so it's not just your test grade, it's you as a person, and it's everything about you. So it's not like, why didn't I do better on that test, it's what's wrong with me?" The subject of study was actually proposed by one of Strauman's grad students who came up with the idea and used the findings to write her dissertation. The study found that girls will brood over possibly failing at something, even if they are knowledgeable about a topic or can perform a task well. Boys tend to be more action-oriented, so do not ruminate over whether or not they know something well enough. They just do it. But Strauman, like many other social scientists, believes that cultural aspects play a major role "from parent's subtle expectations to explicit media messages about unattainable appearance goals."

    While Beauvoir believed that a woman is made, it is not correct to completely rule out the factors that biology plays as to why girls are more sensitive than boys in regard to image and self-definition. Louise Brizendine writes in her book *The Female Brain* that "each hormone state—girlhood, the adolescent years, the dating years, motherhood, and menopause—act as fertilizer for different neurological connections that are responsible for new thoughts, emotions, and interests. Because of the fluctuations that begin as early as three months old and last until after menopause, a woman's neurological reality is not as constant as a man's." This doesn't mean that we are hostages to our hormones or that women cannot hold the same position a man can, it just means that we cannot discount the role that hormones play on the way adolescent girls to grown women see themselves and the world around them.

In 1999 the American Academy of Pediatrics (AAP) came out with a book called *Caring for Your School-Age Child, Ages 5 to 12*. With regard to girls, adolescence, and self-esteem they write that

> In about one-third of girls, a decline in self-esteem becomes pronounced and long-lasting. Sadness, anxiety and eating disorders are more prevalent in girls on the brink of becoming teenagers. As young as the age of 7, many girls start becoming self-critical of their bodies, and up to fifty percent of 9-year-old girls have already tried dieting. Between the ages of 11 and 13, some girls lose much of their emotional strength and spirit. They may develop a crisis in confidence and become depressed. Their optimism dampens, and they become less likely to take chances. By the time girls enter high school, less than one-third of them report being happy with the way they are.

I had a slight problem with this information: one-third of how many girls? The constant use of the word "may" is a precarious word to use, meaning that it could happen or it doesn't. I read this paragraph and felt it just created more cause for panic from parents over their daughters and the changes they go through. But my view changed somewhat after watching an episode on sex, prostitution and teenage girls on the Tyra Banks show. I rarely watch daytime TV, but I found it ironic to come across this particular episode while writing this book. I found myself squirming as girls related stories about feeling ugly and using sex as a way to feel better about themselves. Girls, as young as thirteen, related stories about having sex with men old enough to be their fathers in order to feel beautiful and loved. And these were girls from normal homes with caring mothers.

Given the fact that girls are more sensitive than boys, the exploitation of this sensitivity seems almost criminal. Naomi Wolf, author of the *Beauty Myth*, wrote that the beauty myth is the one last attack against women because it is the one thing that keeps women subjugated to a concept that is not real. There is no "ideal" however much advertisers and the media project such a concept. Raising our little girls to be sexy, based on images they see on television or in magazines is creating an image in their minds that they will constantly feel they need to contend with, thus continuing the cycle of the Mythic Woman.

When I started this chapter, I wrote saying that it is easier said than done to raise our daughters in a different environment than the one prescribed by society. In 1972 with the passing of Title IX legislation which states that "No person in the United States shall, on the basis of sex, be excluded from participation in, be denied the benefits of, or be subjected to discrimination under any education program or activity receiving Federal financial assistance," the groundwork was laid for future females to be able to participate equally in any education or athletic program. This legislation, it was hoped, would push more females to participate in math and science programs, thus changing the myth that they weren't smart enough to do so.

Such legislation is wonderful as it provides opportunity, but it didn't address the underlying social implication of females moving into what was normally perceived as "male territory." I can attest to this from my own experience in high school when a group of girls and I wanted to start a soccer team. The boys had one and the girls wanted one too. The school administration wasn't pleased. The idea received a less than lukewarm response despite it being 1982, ten years since the legislation was passed.

It wasn't that the school didn't have the money or a coach who willingly came forth to offer his time to coach us. It was the social stigma that soccer is a rough sport and girls were too delicate to play. When presenting our case to the school board, we had to show the number of different schools that already had female soccer teams to prove that we would have other teams to play against.

Here we are almost thirty years later and the girls who were students then, are now mothers with their own daughters in high school. Remembering what they went through in high school and the stigma they struggled with, they'd be damned to watch their daughters go through the same thing. I heard this again and again in my conversations with women. We are the moms who keep enforcing the idea into our daughters that they can be anything they want. They just have to work harder than their male counterparts. Stay focused and don't give in. Don't listen to those demons inside your head that tell you you're not good enough. As moms, coaches, and role models, we think we might just be able to create a generation of girls who won't get caught up in the Mythic Woman syndrome. Maybe we can turn that corner. I too believed this to be true until I read Laura Sessions Stepp's book *Unhooked: How Young Women Pursue Sex, Delay Love and Lose at Both*. While I highly recommend every parent to read this book, I was disturbed by what Stepp's research brought to light about having our daughters believe they can have it all. I still believe they can, but sometimes the messages we give as parents and the messages society gives through the media, can cause more harm than good. We want our daughters to be empowered, but at what cost? Stepp's research emphasizes even more that women need to create the roadmap.

Stepp is a reporter for the *Washington Post* and after several reports came in about the "hook up culture" that kids, as young as middle school are involved in, she followed three groups of women for one year, one in high school, one at George Washington University and one at Duke. She did this basically to find out what "hooking up" was about. Dating is out, hooking up is in. And in case parents don't know, hooking up can be anything from kissing to sexual intercourse. There are no strings attached and no expectations. Stepps kept her research to heterosexual girls though hooking up is found in same sex relations as well. What she found was that for women in college, hooking up with a guy is preferred because dating is considered "exhausting." It requires commitment and time that a girl, if she wants to focus on college and a career, doesn't have time for. The philosophy is, if guys can shop around, so can girls. Of course there are some couples that find out they enjoy one another's company and tend to "hang out" when time permits. But it does not mean that they stop hooking up with others, if they so desire, unless it is agreed by the couple that they won't. Yet, considering it is a somewhat expected behavior, trust is difficult for either individual to have when it comes to their partner.

    Hooking up in college often goes hand in hand with the partying that happens on campuses. While this seems to add to the empowerment of women being able to drink, flirt, and sleep with a guy she finds attractive, the consequences of hooking up tend to backfire when alcohol is involved and things go awry. Many of the women Stepp talked to discussed how the whole "game playing" that guys do should be the same for a woman. Guys play the field all the time, why shouldn't girls? And while many independent-minded women would agree with this statement, "one-night stands" just don't always work for women. The college women Stepp interviewed often have misgivings after hooking up with a guy, even though they are conscious of the choice they made, especially when sex is involved. What is supposed to be empowering for young women—the sexual freedom to sleep with a guy without any kind of commitment—just doesn't have the same effect. The result is that many women felt cheated by their own actions. Given that these women are in their early twenties, I wonder if age makes a difference. Could it be possible that because of the lack of life experience these women have, the Mythic Woman has a greater hold versus a forty-year-old woman who has been around the block?

The other factor that makes hooking up less of a win-win situation is "rape." I put the word rape in quotes deliberately because a woman will question whether or not it was rape because of the situation in which she put herself. Stepp's research came across stories of young women who after drinking went back to the guy's place and took off their clothes (giving the impression they were intending to have sex), and then changed their mind and said no, but the guy didn't stop. They didn't report the incident as rape because they had been drinking and they had originally chosen to have sex. Yes, they had said no, but they questioned themselves because they had put themselves in a precarious situation. I don't condone rape, no is no in my book, but, at the same time, why do females put themselves in such situations? This may seem like a heartless question, but it needs to be addressed.

Sex, as many women know, is more emotional for women than it is for men. Part of this is due to the emotional wiring in a woman's brain as it is different than a man's. Scientists have found that parts of the frontal cortex as well as parts of the limbic cortex of a woman's brain are bulkier than in a man's. This may explain why women tend to respond more emotionally than men. Women think things through much more and process information differently than men because of the way we are wired. While we can't explain everything through science, it has been found that female infants look for visual recognition from their mother's face more than male babies. Females are about connection. Hooking up is not about connection. It's about sex. Sex is about connection for most women. It's not necessarily the case for most men.

In a society where myths and images set the standard of how one should be, it is not surprising that many young women look to men and a sexual relationship to validate who they are. So many sexually active teenage girls and young women sleep with a guy because they are afraid the guy won't like them. From the time girls are small, they are fed messages by the media to be sexual and flaunt what they have to be pleasing. They are given ambiguous messages about being strong, but not being vocal: "Don't comment on the sexism." Music and videos show young girls and women taunting young men, giving the impression that young women can play the same game. No one mentions the risks they might run into that will harm them physically, psychologically, or emotionally. If we want to see future generations of women one step closer to equality, we need to think of a different way to get there. We need to define what empowerment means for a woman without continuing the cycle of the Mythic Woman.

A Culture That No Longer Serves Us

One of the challenges I faced while writing this book was reading the research and books written by what the woman's movement has called "radical feminists." I am not sure where the borderline is between a radical feminist and a feminist, but I don't believe I qualify as a radical feminist. I don't think that one sex can live without the other. Nature is not made that way. One sex dominating another doesn't serve our purpose. The thought that it is time to "get back" at the patriarchal system by dominating men is foolish and unrealistic. Patriarchal beliefs—the belief that things originate from the masculine principle (and all it entails), and the thinking that there is no other way of being—has done a lot of damage in the past to the female population, but I don't think only men are to blame for upholding the patriarchal pattern in which we have been living. It is a way of thinking which stems from our culture and, like all ways of thinking, it can be changed. But women have to change first. We need to *see* the culture that surrounds us. As mentioned earlier, the myths that have been part of our history have become part of our psyche. Many women have accepted the myth that this is the way it is and always has been.

We can believe that the culture that we live in today will change with our daughters, but the myths that have kept women from discovering their full potential have been present for hundreds of years. Every generation of women face new challenges because they are walking into a world that has no road map for them to follow; and culture, as it is defined, is "an integrated pattern of knowledge, belief, and behavior." If we do not change the beliefs that women have subjected themselves to, we cannot change the behavior that comes from those beliefs. More importantly, we have handed our identity and our lives over to a culture that no longer serves us. When did our own inner self or "beingness" suddenly become something not worth fighting for? Is it really okay that so many women in this country suffer from some type of self-esteem issue? Or that 1 out of 8 suffers from depression, which is twice as much as men? We can contribute some of it to the biological changes the female body goes through and the lifestyles we live, but I wonder if the severity of depression would be less if women knew who they were and what they wanted from their lives. The only way to do this is by finding one's Authentic Self. In the end, no one can tell us who we are, but there are steps that can be taken to help us get there. One way is to become aware of how women are perceived in today's culture.

The culture that surrounds women is also dependent upon race, education, and economic and social class. I would love to go into the dynamics of all these factors, but there are other women more qualified who have written about it from an experiential and sociological perspective. I mention these cultural influences because they impact how a woman is perceived and how she perceives herself. However, no matter what ethnic background a woman comes from, no matter what her economic standing is, no matter how much education she has, women know they are the oppressed gender. Some will talk about it openly because it is something they are very aware of, while others will talk about that "dreaded word" as though it is the plague. As a gender, women are oppressed; and within this gender, there are different levels of oppression. For instance, the oppression perceived by Hispanic women will be different than the oppression perceived by Black women; likewise for White women versus Black women. In fact if you talk to some non-White women, they will tell you they don't believe White women are oppressed at all. What is oppression to some is not oppression to another, especially when the opportunities are so different for so many women.

One of the drawbacks during the women's movement was the disagreement about what constituted oppression. The oppression I would like to focus on is the oppression found in the female psyche that applies to all women and which hinders her from finding her Authentic Self. Perhaps one day, we can use this as common ground to empathize with each other and work to uplift *all* women, while being sensitive to each woman's life experience. For me personally, I find being able to experience another woman's culture as a great life lesson. It is an opportunity that every woman should take advantage of, because we learn not only how different we are, but how, at a certain level, we are all connected.

Paulo Freire, in his book *The Pedagogy of the Oppressed*, characterized certain behaviors as the "consciousness of the oppressed." Freire was an exile from Brazil who lived in Chile for five years. His masterpiece was written after careful observation and analysis of himself and those around him who were oppressed and disempowered. Granted, women in the US are no longer boxed off from the world. As a population, we have empowered each other by fighting for causes we believe in—such as daycare, family leave, and domestic violence legislation to name a few. We've supported each other when we felt "no one else really understands," and we have spent hours being the sounding board for one another despite our differences. But as individual human beings, we still maintain the mindset or the "consciousness of the oppressed," as Freire called it, despite all the rights and freedoms we have fought for and attained.

Freire characterized the "consciousness of the oppressed" as those who have "internalized the image of the oppressor and adopted his guidelines." Whether we agree with it or not, we internalize and follow certain images and myths instead of stepping back and questioning whether such images and modes really serve and help us define who we are. We allow the images, myths, and societal expectations to oppress us. We become, as Freire writes, "divided beings," "contradictory," because we want to try to live according to the guidelines of society, even if it runs against our own inner sense of being. This is why we say "yes" when we want to say "no" and why we suffer through pleasing others without any consideration of ourselves.

Another characteristic Freire writes about is self-deprecation. While this is typical in most humans, as we all have doubts about our own capabilities, women are often more self-deprecating than men, suffer more often from depression and mood swings, and have a higher rate of physical self-destruction. (Not suicide, but destructive behaviors of the body, mind, and emotional well-being.) This self-deprecation leads to emotional dependence. Freire writes that oppressed cultures often don't know what they want. They don't trust their own judgment and worry whether the decision they make will be the one that suits those around them (or the culture that oppresses them). Such anguish leads to anxiety, depression, a false sense of self, and feeling of *ennui*, i.e. boredom, weariness, dissatisfaction.

Two factors that are tied together in the oppressed mindset are fear and control. Noam Chomsky, a social critic, political activist, and intellectual, has written about how big businesses make the rules and set the standards in society and that by instilling fear in people, businesses control them. This is true of society in general, but with regard to women, advertising companies have set the standard about how to be sexy and desirable, a good mother and wife, and a good daughter—by making the right choices. Watch any channel on TV and, depending on the program, there will be innumerable amounts of ads directed toward women. The latest ad by Gerber is to ensure moms buy their baby food because it is enriched with omega-3 which contains the essential fatty acid known as docosahexaenoic acid (DHA). DHA is passed onto the fetus when developing in the mother and is also present in breast milk. It helps the brain development in unborn babies; however

Gerber is now adding the fatty acid to their baby food stating that it helps brain development in toddlers (and for goodness sake, what kind of mother are you if you don't want your child's brain to develop?) The advertisements promote the latest finding or fad. Omega-3 is the new one. I don't remember buying formula enriched with omega-3 when my daughter and son were infants and I don't think they are suffering brain damage or the inability to think. DHA was added to baby formula in 2002. But new mothers will worry and will do what the latest ad tells them to, because like any normal healthy mother, they want to do what is best for their baby This is just one example, but the advertisements use language in such a way to instill fear and the "what if" factor.

  I find myself watching cable news channels less and less because I can't stand the way the newscasters address me, the viewer. The world is going to hell in a hand basket and there is no recourse for any of us except to give in to the anxiety of it all. It doesn't matter if you watch CNN, MSNBC, or Fox News, the world is falling apart. Newscasters almost rant at the viewer, trying to incite them to get angry. I remember once thinking that the commentator was going to pop a blood vessel because he was getting so riled up over an issue. Some time, when you are watching television, count how many negative stories they report and how many positive ones. Then watch the ads. Reality TV does the same thing except the ads are geared toward women. Women, through advertising, are told they are fat, dull, smelly, and dirty. We need better hygiene products, better hair care products, and we need colon cleansing products so we can lose weight. And when we are done with beautifying and perfecting ourselves, we need to clean our houses, our kids, our clothes. Everything must be germ free. (We have got to be the most sterile country on the planet!) But we need better cleaning products that clean faster so we can clean more in less time.

I used to think that television ads basically helped sell products for companies, but as I watched carefully, I became aware of how many ads were geared toward women "needing" things to become "extraordinary," while men only needed Viagra. I haven't seen an ad for jock itch next to an ad for menstrual pads or tampons. Why is something that is personal for women advertised a thousand times, while for the longest time no one knew what Rogaine did? It initially wasn't mentioned that it was for male balding until women's Rogaine came out. But the ads that are directed toward women are about improvement, subconsciously telling us that we aren't good enough. The worst ones are the ads for depression and senility medication. (Women are not only more vulnerable to depression than men, but to Alzheimers as well.)

Advertising and media not only play on women's psyches, but distort how we perceive each other in relationships. *Can't Buy My Love*, Jean Kilbourne's book published in 1999, exposes the exploitation of women through advertising and the media. As a former model, Kilbourne became aware of the image versus the reality concept and while her book focuses more on how advertisers push cigarette smoking and alcohol among young women, she raises some thought-provoking ideas about how advertising changes our perception. I wonder if I should even use the word "change" as we really know no other way of viewing the world because our perception is based on what we see. If, for the majority of our lives, we see only what the media and advertisers want us to see, we know little else.

Kilbourne writes that advertising contributes to our throwaway attitude. We are so used to instant gratification that working for anything—an intimate relationship, a promotion, conception of a child, a house—whatever the case maybe, we want it right away. In the US, our society works to provide this immediacy. Companies try to figure out how to provide the best product so that they can keep up with the expectation they have created in consumers to have everything as soon as possible. I see this in myself when I call or email someone and expect a response right away. (And I am from a generation of landlines and no answering machine!) We don't know how to wait, we lack patience, and as long as we are brainwashed to believe that we need everything right away, there will be no slowing down until nature comes along and does it for us.

Our throwaway attitude has created a number of different problems within our society. Not only do we have a need for immediacy, we look at the image as the reality and we need the image to *be* the reality. We judge people based on characters on TV. The qualities we find in TV characters are qualities we want in the men or women we meet. There is a huge problem here: Reality TV is not reality. It is reality on TV which is mocked up and produced to make money. Sadly for some people, their life becomes a soap opera with one bad choice after another being made; like TV they need to have drama. Unfortunately, life in the REAL world is not as exciting. Relationships with other people take time to grow, especially intimate ones.

When we don't get something we want, we either choose differently, or we use some other means to make sure we get what we want. With regard to women and relationships, Kilbourne writes that as women we often have an image in our head of what our partner should be like. We have our list. Often the people we meet and the qualifications on the list don't add up, so we move on. Or we expect that the person we commit to—who has some drawbacks--will change once we are with them (because we are so influential), but they don't and we can't figure out why. If the adjusting didn't take place while dating, it isn't going to change once the relationship is legalized. (This is something to remember when you set the "Marry me or else" ultimatum.)

This need for immediate gratification may explain the hookup culture that has slowly become prevalent in our high schools and on our college campuses. It may also explain the number of people who decide to go outside of their marriage in search of the connection they originally found in their significant other. Peggy Vaughan, in her book *The Monogamy Myth*, approximates that 60% of husbands and 40% of wives will have an affair at some point in their marriage. While other studies say that this is a high estimate, marital affairs have, according to some, almost doubled in the last twenty years. Vaughan's website "AskPeggy.com" mentions that there are three reasons a person will have a relationship outside of marriage, one of them being "societal factors." Within this category she lists how affairs are glamorized on television, in soap operas, and romance novels. The affairs among movies stars or reality TV personalities are also glamorized. Look at how much coverage the never-ending divorce between Jon and Kate Gosselin got compared to the separation and divorce of Al and Tipper Gore. Another factor Kilbourne lists, is the objectification of women: "Over and over, the message to men is that the good life includes a parade of sexy women in their lives. Women inadvertently buy into this image and strive to achieve it."

Interestingly, it has always been thought that men more than women have affairs. Historically this has been true, but women are slowly catching up with men, leveling out the percentages. In fact while researching about married women having affairs, the first search engine that came up was for the Ashley Madison agency. It's an agency that promotes "discreet dating" with a motto that says "Life is short. Have an affair." It apparently has 4.5 million members and has been advertised on *The View*, *Ellen*, *Good Morning America*, and *Dr. Phil*. I guess this is such an accepted behavior that there's actually a business for it! When trying to research what it is that women are looking for when having an affair, the first response is sex and the second is recognition, i.e. attention, feeling desired, the excitement of doing something considered "taboo," etc. I wonder if the need to keep finding something to liven up one's life would diminish if women felt satisfied with their inner sense of being. I also wonder whether doing so would strengthen their need to make choices that are not easy—such as ending a relationship that no longer benefits them or face the painful issue of a deteriorating relationship.

But it is obvious, based on the behavior of women, that there is a search for something more than what today's society is offering them. Women are trying to change the culture around them, but don't seem sure what that change should be. Perhaps by looking at some of the myths that we incorporate into our lives we can find a way to create our own culture. A culture where we have the courage to voice our opinions; not struggle with our self-esteem (which in turn makes us take a backseat to our own goals and dreams), and where our bodies and how we look, are not the first things on our minds.

Some myths dominate our lives more than others. You may see yourself in some of these myths and not so much in others. Some women are not afraid to say what's on their minds while others swallow their words. Some women are very self-assured with their bodies while others feel uncomfortable in their own skin. While you may not see yourself in one of the myths, your girlfriends might. And if we are going to change the culture we live in, we have to do it together. The way to do this is no different than how we come to each other's rescue when times are difficult. Girlfriends provide comfort, solace, and strength for one another, sometimes without even saying a word. We need to do that for each other to fight these myths. We need to fight the battle for every woman and not just ourselves. It is slowly being done now with movements that push for real women in real bodies being displayed on magazine covers, or models that come forward to openly talk about how unhealthy the modeling industry can be for a woman's body, all in the name of beauty.

    On a personal note, I have watched myself with some of these myths. Some are more difficult to fight than others, depending on one's upbringing. For instance, if all your life you've been told that all that matters are your looks, fighting the myth that you aren't pretty enough, or thin enough, becomes a constant nag in the back of your head. I struggle with not being smart enough and no matter what I do, or how many degrees I get, it's still a struggle. But when you are told all your life, "It's okay, you'll get by on your looks," the myth takes over your whole sense of being. We need to be incredibly careful about *what* we say to our daughters, *how* we say things to our daughters, and have our sisters, mothers, daughters, and girlfriends remind us when we allow the myth to rule our lives.

The Myth of Keeping Silent

I always think of Edith Bunker from the 1970s show *All in the Family*, when I think about the myth of keeping silent. I remember learning the word "stifle" from hearing it on the show and using it on someone and almost getting slapped. I couldn't understand why it was used on a television show, but I couldn't use the word. As I got older I realized the word wasn't for children, or females in general, to use. It was for adults to use, mainly male adults toward females. And while the writers and producers of the show used Archie Bunker's character as a parody of the behavior and thinking of chauvinistic men, the character of Edith revealed the accommodating that women did to put up with chauvinistic behavior. It was usually Edith who, despite her being a "ding bat" (according to Archie), had the upper hand. However she always made Archie feel he ruled the roost as she quietly went about defusing a heated situation.

Women have often been the movers and shakers behind the scenes. Not able to hold public office for many years and then, at times, being the "token" woman on a board or in some places of employment in the name of equality, women have had to find ways to work around situations while not creating too much commotion. This is one of the reasons women are so adept at volunteer work. We know how to manage with little or no resources or support and we are determined to get the job done. We quietly go about doing what we do. The key word here is "quietly" because that used to be how we were expected to be: quiet.

The silencing of women has been explored in the writings of many feminist literary writers. Martha J. Cutter in her book *Unruly Tongue* analyzes the work of women writers from the years 1850 to 1930 such as Fanny Fern, Louisa May Alcott, Harriet Wilson, Kate Chopin, Charlotte Perkins Gilman, and other writers. She also explores the concept of identity, and voice and its transformation from domestic to maternal or feminine to metalinguistic/ethnic voice. The metalinguistic voice seeks to break the boundaries created by masculine versus feminine/dominant versus subjective dichotomy. In some communities in this country, English is slowly moving in this direction—to be less gender-centered, more universal and encompassing—but more work still needs to be done. Despite this, women are still working through overcoming the silencing of their sex and the fears that stem from it while trying to find their voice.

With regard to silence, there are two kinds. There is the silence found in prayer or meditation, where we willingly allow the silence to envelop us and become part of us. In this silence we find strength and clarity; such silence basically gives our souls a chance to breathe. The other type of silence happens through coercion. It is the silence put upon us by outside events or forces. It is silence due to an inability to express ourselves or communicate. The inability may not start through our own doing, but we become so used to not expressing ourselves or communicating, it becomes part of who we are. It is this type of silence with which we are more familiar.

As many women are aware, the ability to "be silent and know one's place" was a qualification many families looked for in a bride for their son. Silence was synonymous with a good woman because she would be obedient and not cause embarrassment to her new family. This imposition to be quiet was promoted through religion and then enforced by law with a woman having to speak through her husband or a male family member. Women who spoke back were considered unruly and at times punished. Eventually silence becomes a way of protecting ourselves from others. And while this may not be prevalent in the US, it is still happening in other countries and in other cultures around the world.

In cases of abuse, infidelity, chemical dependency, or a situation outside of the "norm" of society, we use silence to cover our shame or embarrassment. We are governed by the myth of perfection and to not uphold that myth leads to self-esteem issues where we believe that silence is better than expressing our pain. We begin to make excuses as to why it is better to be silent: we don't want to offend anyone, we don't want to say something stupid, we think what we say won't add value, we feel we don't know how to say what we need to say, or we think someone else will say what we want to say. And we are so afraid of the reaction we think we will get if we express ourselves.

In the end, we need to believe and understand that our ability to express ourselves is a human right. In fact it is a need of every human being because expression is our way of showing others who we are. When we shut that part of ourselves off, we become stagnant emotionally and spiritually. We lack the energy we require from others to exist and we become shells of ourselves, thus continuing the Mythic Woman status. We have the face and body, but there is no light in our eyes and we feel hollow within.

Audre Lourde writes in her essay, *The Transformation of Silence into Language and Action*, "And of course I am afraid, because the transformation of silence into language and action is an act of self-revelation, and that always seems fraught with danger." Coming forward and standing up for what you believe in allows the world to question you. And history has shown that we humans tend to be a ruthless species when it comes to questioning each other. Some women find it overwhelming when asked to explain why they believe what they believe, especially when under hostile conditions. I have watched this time and again. We often become so tongue-tied that we hide within ourselves, believing our silence will protect us, but it never will. Think of the number of women who throughout history searched for their Authentic Self or identity, but did not have the right to express who they were. It would seem almost disrespectful and selfish to them to have that right today and not use it. As a community, we all have something to teach. We all have a desire we wish to achieve. We all have causes we want to fight for. The only way to do this is by putting ourselves out there and speaking from the heart.

Many women say it is difficult for them to vocalize what they want to say, so they find another medium to express themselves. There are scores of women who write poetry, draw and paint, create pottery, photograph, dance, or even make quilts to express who they are. As a population we've been doing this for hundreds of years, and yet there are still many women who choose the wall of silence over stepping out because they feel that they will be misunderstood.

In her book, *You Just Don't Understand,* Deborah Tannen addresses this issue. Through research and interviews she studied the different ways men and women communicate and related those nuances in her book. Some of her examples are situations that we've all been through, and it is almost comical to read. Having the ability to step back and see the various situations from a distance, make the solutions seem very easy.

One major problem women have in communicating (not that men don't, but this book is about us) is our indirectness. As mentioned before, we often apologize before we state our opinion or are direct in our speaking, instead of just saying what we need to say. We do this because we are concerned about how the other person is going to feel. We always want to soften the blow. We also have a tendency to not want to inconvenience anyone so we will ask things indirectly, hoping others will agree with us. Tannen uses the example of a husband and wife on a long distance drive; the wife asks her husband if he wants coffee and he says, "No." What he doesn't realize is that his wife wants coffee and is upset that he doesn't ask her. Of course, men have gotten a little smarter in all of this and now know they need to ask us what we want. And generations are slowly changing to where women will now say, "Hey can we stop? I need to get some coffee."

We women run things through our heads over and over before we come out and just say what we want. I find myself doing this when I have to bring up a topic that has previously caused strong emotions either in my husband or me. I also have a tendency to ruminate about a decision, not wanting to inconvenience anyone. But as many women put it, men tend to be resolvers. They want to fix (or end) the situation instead of just being a sounding board. I often think this quality is because of our patriarchal society, as I have a few girlfriends that work in the corporate world, and follow this behavior. It stems from the "time is money" concept.

One time I was driving with two dear friends to a winter weekend getaway. Unfortunately, it began snowing and the two-lane country road we were driving on was covered with drifting snow. Living in Chicago most of my life, I am used to snowy roads, but after thirty minutes of driving thirty miles an hour, I found myself getting annoyed. I was sure there had to be a better road to get to the same place. So I commented that we needed to find another road. One friend said, "Well let's wait, maybe it will get better. We're out in the country so it will be the same everywhere." The other friend who worked in a dominantly male environment began checking the GPS on her phone for a better way and began giving different options. I found myself laughing at how different we all were in our approach to the problem; it made me realize I wasn't enjoying these two beautiful women that I loved being with. I was worried about getting to the destination. The other two caught on immediately because we often talked about enjoying the moment. Needless to say, I stopped worrying about time and just allowed myself to enjoy them. We had a great weekend despite the drifting snow, the lousy roads, and the cold weather.

In the US, especially, we are about efficiency and effectiveness, which can have its drawbacks. Women process things differently and want to find the solution to a problem by working through what they are feeling. This is why women talk to their female friends before coming to a conclusion about something. For those who focus on efficiency and being effective, "processing," as it is called in counseling, seems to be a waste of time, especially when there is a deadline. However, there is a difference between speaking up and hashing out differences than not considering anyone's feelings and coming to a resolution that works for a few people. One method is about the means of coming to a resolution and the other is about the resolution itself. This doesn't mean hours need to be spent talking about how to solve something, but individual growth happens when we allow ourselves to express what we feel.

There has been a lot written about this and while we are still trying to figure out how to come a level of communication that works for both sexes, there are things women can do to strengthen their ability to speak up for themselves. Granted this is much more difficult in cases of abuse and dysfunction, but the feeling of being able to stand in one's place and have people know what you feel regarding a situation is empowering. And your silence, in the end, will not protect you.

The Myth of the Ugly Duckling

We all know the story of the ugly duckling, the cygnet getting mixed into a family of ducks and wondering why it does not look like them. The cygnet eventually turns into a beautiful swan, but until it sees its reflection in the water, it believes it is ugly as it does not look like its brothers and sisters, i.e. it does not follow the "accepted pattern." The moral of the story is about the uniqueness of every being and the beauty within.

Such a story falls on deaf ears in so many cultures today, especially as our gender is used to set the standard of what is in and what is out, who is "beautiful" and who is "just average," from the time we are born. I used to laugh when newborn babies were entered into contests—has anyone ever seen an ugly newborn? The concept seems ridiculous. But we base our looks on what advertisers and the media set as the standard and go from there, instead of realizing we are all genetically unique. We come in all shapes and sizes, with different skin tones and textures. Spending thousands of dollars to modify ourselves to look like the latest superstar is futile. What is "in" now will be "out" in another six months, if not three. And honestly, do we all really want to look alike?

In her book *The Beauty Myth: How Images of Beauty are Used against Women*, Naomi Wolf brought to light the power that the myth of beauty has over women. Published in 1991, the book, and much of what it discusses, still rings true today. Wolf asks the question, "Who decides what is beautiful?" She discusses what drives women to accept the standards decided by others when they know full well that they are impossible standards to attain. The myth that beauty or what is considered beautiful, is equivalent to acceptance, availability, attractiveness, and therefore power, often leaves young girls and women disillusioned and despondent. Women, young and old, who follow the set standard and make all the "required" changes, wonder what they are doing wrong and why such changes aren't working. Why can't they find eternal happiness in the latest fashion, hairstyle, color, bigger breasts, luscious lips, collagen, and Botox injections? Why aren't more men/women attracted to them?

Wolf writes that we are "in the midst of a violent backlash against feminism that uses images of female beauty as a political weapon against women's advancement: the beauty myth. As women released themselves from the feminine mystique of domesticity, the beauty myth took over its lost ground . . .The contemporary backlash is so violent because the ideology of beauty is the last one remaining of the old feminine ideologies that still has the power to control those women whom second wave feminism would have otherwise made relatively uncontrollable. . ."

Beauty was another "qualification" a woman needed in order to be considered for marriage. A beautiful woman for a man represented greater power. And according to Wolf, "the qualities that a given period calls beautiful in women are merely symbols of the female behavior that that period considers desirable: The beauty myth is always actually prescribing behavior and not appearance." So, while beauty was considered a qualification for marriage, what beauty really represented was the demeanor of a woman, did she obey, speak softly and sparingly, take care of her duties without complaint, did she have good health, etc.

In 2004 Dove globally launched the "Campaign for Real Beauty" to advertise that beauty was much deeper than the surface of one's skin. Their message was loud and clear: *beauty lies within*. And the ad used women of all ages, shapes, sizes, and skin tone to show that it didn't matter what you looked like, what mattered was who you were inside and it was up to women to define beauty themselves. It was a promotion in self-esteem whose goal was to reach five million women worldwide by 2010.

No different is the campaign by Proctor and Gamble called "My Black is Beautiful"—which was about black women defining for themselves what is beautiful instead allowing outside images to dictate it. Both of these campaigns are incredibly important at a time when less than 2% of the women in the US feel they are beautiful, while 81% of the female population is aware that advertisers set the standard of what is beautiful. Most women are also aware that they can never achieve the standard because it is computerized. But why do women feel they need to be beautiful? Can anyone really tell what is beautiful? After all, who defines it?

The concept of the beauty myth and what it really means has created quite a stir since Wolf's book was originally published. While the fashion industry sets the standard, it is a standard that even Hollywood stars are beginning to push against. More often than not, some of the highest paid actresses are popping the mythic bubble behind the "Hollywood stars beauty." In the March 2009 issue of *In Style* magazine, Sandra Bullock was asked by a young woman from New York City, "What do you tell a girl who feels ugly because she's not blond or doesn't have a thin nose?" Bullock responds, "Welcome to my broken nose!" She goes on to mention that she was never considered a beauty, was rejected in high school because she wasn't big-breasted, and was "awkward and sad." Despite her mother telling her to be original, Bullock points out that she didn't realize what that meant until she tried to fit in and be like everyone else. Once she jumped into the pond and tried to be like the rest of the fish, she lost her own identity, her own uniqueness, and quickly jumped out.

In the same issue of *In Style*, on the section called "Beauty Talk," actress Halle Berry divulged "her best kept beauty secrets" which were that "less is more." She states, "When I wear too much makeup, I feel like a man in drag." And whether it is her actual quote or not, what caught my eye the most was a quote under Berry's photo which says, "I think the more you get in touch with yourself, the better you look." Thank goodness someone is doing their homework. Can we have a million more magazines push this concept? Perhaps if we get more women to believe and speak this truth, then maybe we can influence our daughters to believe it too.

However, the beauty myth is ingrained in us from the time we are little girls and while we all know that we need to break out of the vicious cycle, the only way to do so is to begin feeling comfortable in our own skin. I was given an incredible gift when I was invited to live in India at a time when looks and fashion were not focused on as much as they are today. (This was over twenty years ago and things in India have changed drastically. Unfortunately, the East seems to be the West nowadays.) But the fact that my focus shifted away from my body and what I looked liked, to becoming aware of my thoughts and what I was capable of learning, gave me a sense of empowerment and identity that would have been difficult to connect with in later years.

Just like Halle Berry's quote: when we begin to know ourselves, there is a confidence within that cannot be weakened. We feel content with who we are, so we stop looking for outside standards. We come to terms with our facial features and our body shape and grow to love what nature gave us. We may not always be pleased with the changes our bodies go through, but we accept that it is part of who we are. We know within what it is we need to change in our life and why—and it isn't to follow some standard, but with the intent to better our lives and keep ourselves healthy—and no matter what situation we find ourselves in, or the circle we become part of, we always come back to that knowing and strength within because it is our Authentic Self.

The Myth of the Super Mom

There are two sides to this myth, both of which were created by society. The first was that a stay-at-home mom was "just a mom," who didn't have any skills, didn't contribute anything financially to society, and therefore her role didn't account for anything. (This is a rather crude way of stating this.) To combat this myth, a second view was created by various populations, thinkers, media, and advertisers, in order to please women and make them feel important. Women were no longer housewives, but were "domestic engineers." Details were kept of the number of jobs a stay-at-home mom did during the day and if she were paid, how much she would earn. I think the last time I checked, it was up to $70,000.

The title of "domestic engineer" was to give the impression that women were more than just housewives. It was a response to the backlash women gave to the impression had that stay-at-home moms were airheads and that running a household was nothing compared to the work done in a company outside of the house. However, the domestic engineer slowly morphed into the Super Mom, a standard that only "real" moms could attain. Somewhere along the way, someone upped the ante. Nowadays, moms or dads are not "good" parents if they don't have their kids in sports, tutoring classes, and music classes, plus provide them with all the latest gadgets that create the image of being good parents. There is a standard set. Stay-at-home parents need to be as busy as a CEO in a corporation and the employees are their children. Forget about nurturing and chocolate chip cookies, we're on the fast track.

The understanding of what it means to nurture our children needs to be brought back into parenting. Nurturing has nothing to do with keeping our kids busy or keeping up with the Joneses. It has to do with being available for our children, guiding them through the ups and downs of friendships and heartbreaks, teaching them resilience, self-reliance, responsibility, and accountability. Too many kids today no longer know how to entertain themselves during the summer because they are so busy during the school year. The constant activity of school, friends, sports, and other activities often do not teach them accountability or responsibility, because parents (more often moms than dads) take on the extra burdens as a sign of being a better parent. Parents are the ones who keep track of practices, uniforms, forms, and so on. For some reason, and I was guilty of this, we don't allow our children to fail because we think it reflects on us as moms.

The myth of being the Super Mom, that by keeping our kids constantly busy and attending to their every need, can actually have a detrimental effect on them because, like us, they can become so caught up in their own lives that little else matters. What is happening in the world, how they will be affected by it, and how they are connected to it, doesn't seem to concern them. This isn't with all teenagers, but more often than not, I hear parents say that teens today seem more self-centered than they were as teenagers. I honestly think it is due to the immediacy of everything in their lives, including the response they get from us as their parents.

Combating the images and hype of how we are supposed to be as moms is often more difficult than we realize. Sometimes we take on more, trying to either prove to ourselves or to others that we can do more, because we think we are "less than." I remember the utter sadness I felt when I realized I had to quit my job to stay home with my kids. I love my kids dearly, but I also loved the stimulation of my job. In the end, it just wasn't worth the paycheck I handed over for childcare and the anxiety I felt everyday wondering if they were taken care of well enough. To this day, I don't regret the choice or the sacrifices my husband and I made for me to stay home.

When my kids got a little older, I went back to work. While the job was full-time, I worked part-time hours in the office and the rest of it at home. I kept thinking if other moms could do it, I could do it too. After all, I was educated and had worked hard to get my degrees. To show I could do more (and that I was a Super Mom), I got involved with starting a Parent-Teacher Organization (PTO) at my daughter's middle school. There had never been one before and I had a chance to put my Masters degree in public administration to good use. While it was one of the most rewarding times, it was one of the most exhausting. I did get to spend more time with my kids as I was at the school during and after school hours, in the evenings, and on weekends with one event after another. (The employees at Taco Bell got to know us on a first name basis.) It was time together, but not quality time.

But the whole thing was a balancing act. One reason it was even possible was because every board member did their own individual job and followed through with their responsibilities. We did help one another when needed, but our board was made up of stay-at-home moms and working moms, and trust was what held us together. We supported each other, laughed about how we felt like we were going around the bend due to our commitment to our kids and husbands, or how few hours of sleep we got. We got stressed out about the household expenses we incurred from eating out, the lack of home cooked meals for our kids, the hours our kids spent doing homework on the cafeteria floor and not in the comfort of their own home, and the politics of the school administration. We laughed until we cried, mourned for the students who lost a parent on our watch, got angry over the firing of a good teacher, and kept each other going. I pray every board, no matter what the organization or business, gets the chance to feel such camaraderie and unity when working with each other.

I will never regret the activity or stress I went through to achieve what we did. It was good to see moms and dads volunteer for PTO sponsored events, but we constantly emphasized our inclusiveness, our openness to have others involved, and the importance of how our actions were providing better resources for our school so our kids could have a better education. But once my term ended, Super Mom ended too. Yet, despite retiring and passing the torch on to others, I got pulled into meetings with the following board as a consultant whenever they felt things were not going well. I didn't mind this as I was a founding member, had helped set up the bylaws and create a vision, and I still felt an obligation toward the organization.

One of the bylaws we had was that a member could not hold a board position if their child or children did not attend the school. We did this specifically to keep parents, grandparents, and guardians involved while keeping people unconnected with the school off the board and away from handling the thousands of dollars that ran through our PTO. Unfortunately, not everyone plays by the same rules and not everyone feels that the bylaws, which are created to protect an organization, are *not* there for one's own personal welfare.

The following board came across a situation where one mom insisted on finishing her term (which ran two years) on the board despite not having a child in the school the second year of her term. The board was willing to allow her to stay on except that there were other problems with this mom. She unfortunately suffered from what the other board members termed "the ultra-Super Mom complex." To compensate for things not going well in her life, this mom felt she needed to have her finger in every pie. So despite being in charge of one committee, she insisted on helping with another committee where no help was needed. When she was responsible for a particular event, she was busy doing something else and could not be found. In decisions where her input was not necessary, she insisted on giving her feedback. Her kids were involved in several activities so she was often unable to follow through with things she committed to, and yet, she kept up the appearance that nothing was wrong while everyone else on the board was getting annoyed. There are only so many hours in a day and so many activities in which one can participate. As mentioned earlier, it is all a balancing act.

  The Super Mom complex is nothing new, but it is something to be aware of as women living in the "age of anxiety," as Judith Warner calls it. There are different levels of the Super Mom, but the ultra-Super Mom is the desperate housewife on amphetamines. We try as much as possible to keep up the standards of the perfect mom. We give everything to our kids and everyone else around us, but leave little or nothing for ourselves. In her book *Perfect Madness: Motherhood in the Age of Anxiety*, Warner writes that "the demon images of perfect motherhood that haunt us are very largely our own creation." We follow whatever is the latest craze; not wanting to miss out or be categorized as anything but the perfect mom. And I will tell you it is addicting. I get a small thrill when my kids tell me I am a "cool mom." But being the Super Mom, like the Super Woman, can have its downside.

  Warner writes that "too many of us now allow ourselves to be defined by motherhood and direct every ounce of our energy into our children . . . when we lose ourselves in our mommy selves, we experience this loss as depression. When we disempower ourselves in our mommy selves, we experience this weakness as anxiety. When we desexualize ourselves in our mommy selves, it leads us to feel dead in our skin." We think we are just tired, but we are drained because we are using all our energy trying to live up to a standard that just doesn't exist.

  In the April 2009 issue of the *Atlantic Monthly* Hanna Rosin writes in her article "The Case Against Breastfeeding," that in "certain overachieving circles, breastfeeding is no longer a choice—it's a no-exceptions requirement, the ultimate badge of responsible parenting." Rosin questions whether breastfeeding, which according to the American Medical Association has little impact on a baby's development versus formula, isn't "this generation's vacuum cleaner—an instrument of misery that mostly just keeps women down." This doesn't mean women who breastfeed should stop—I, for one, believe breastfeeding has its benefits no matter what anyone says—but Rosin wonders if the push that women *must* breastfeed is just another form of paranoia which adds to the mothering anxiety. Sadly, mothers themselves keep the battle camps alive with their inclusive-exclusive attitude of who breastfeeds and who doesn't. The myth of the Super Mom rides again.

 As mentioned before, the Super Mom Complex is no different than the Superwoman Complex. The focus is just different. The Superwoman Complex is derived from the belief that we need to help and take care of everyone else's problems. We make everyone else's issues our own, adding nothing but chaos to our lives. This doesn't mean we should not help a friend when they ask. It does mean that we should not enable them. And as women, we do have a reputation of having a soft heart. We will keep bailing out our friends and family, thinking if we help them "one more time," it might make a difference. Like the Superwoman, the Super Mom will not allow her children to fail because she takes it as her own failure. And good girls don't fail because they are supposed to be perfect.

The Myth of Power and Control

When I was in my teens I used to think of a powerful woman as a rebel. But the image I had of a rebel was a person being in someone's face, confrontational, loud, and overbearing. (It's funny because I am only 5'1" and for me to be overbearing or in someone's face, I would have to stand on a stepladder.) But the image is one of instilling fear in another person. As I got older, I realized these images were no different than what I had seen on television. It is the image used in our country and in others to show what power means. We use it in our military, corporate executives of many companies use it on their managers, and managers use it on their employees. As parents we use it on our children. And the media through music, videos, and movies convinces us that by instilling fear in others, we are powerful. When we are powerful, we can control people because they fear us.

With this image of power it is no wonder that women tend to shirk at the word. In her book *If Women Ruled the World*, Dee Dee Myers interviewed the late Anita Roddick, founder of The Body Shop, who said that women basically don't like power because we've seen what it has done to men and our world and we want "no bloody part of it." Roddick stated that women like how power creates moral influence and the ability to bring about change, but "until women want to reclaim the notion of power, I think it's going to be quite hard."

The myth behind power is that there is only one image of power to follow, and that is the image we've been handed by a patriarchal society. We think by following that image, others will know we are powerful. But that is not true. It is by knowing our Authentic Self and finding our own sense of power that we will have the ability to change what power truly means and no longer shirk at the word. However, we can only do this by bringing control into our lives.

As mentioned earlier, control is often thought about in reference to power when it is looked at as a form of oppression. However, if we look at control as a type of discipline, the word takes on a very different meaning. Yoga, which is so popular in this country now, takes discipline. You have to do it regularly in order to see the results. Discipline comes from the Latin word *discipulus*, meaning "pupil" or "student." In yoga, we become students of yoga. In the study of our life, we become students of ourselves or of our own lives. Like any student, we cannot learn if we are pulled in a thousand different directions. We have to set boundaries and—sadly for some women—we have to *learn* to say NO. We have to stand up for ourselves and become disciplined about the choices we make. Most importantly we need to do all of this without GUILT. When we are able to do this, we have more control over our lives and live from our own inner power. We direct our lives. We cannot make changes in our life without taking control of it. As women what we fear is the image we've been given of the woman who is powerful, or in control of her own life, and the beliefs that come with that image. Power doesn't have to be "in your face." In reality, women are already very powerful and often we don't even know it.

Saul Alinsky, in his book *Rules for Radicals*, defines power as the "ability, whether physical, mental, or moral, to act." Looked at from this definition, women are very powerful people as we are constantly acting at all levels, most of the time without any recognition. It is the lack of recognition that makes us feel we are powerless. For much of the work we do, whether it is sitting on a PTO board, managing a baseball team, raising money for a neighbor whose child has cancer, or making dinner for a family going through crisis, these are things that are not recognized on a larger basis. We are recognized by the people we help, the organizations we volunteer for, the school programs we give countless hours to, but we're neither on the cover of a magazine nor do we make the five o'clock news. And we don't expect any recognition or reward. We just do what needs to be done. The most rewarding but unrecognized work that many women do is mothering. Mothering is also an incredibly powerful job, because we mold and provide the world a future population where we teach children how to think, how to get along with one another, how to care for each other, and, hopefully, how to become contributing members to society in a positive way.

I think the myth of power and control is one of the hardest myths to overcome because women are so used to living their lives for others. In Naomi Wolf's 1993 book *Fire with Fire: The New Female Power and How It Will Change the 21st Century*, she writes, "Women can't change the world until they can become comfortable with using power, and with understanding how powerful they already are. Self-esteem is not limited to feeling confident about oneself. The step past that is feeling confident about one's rights and ability to change the world." So, how about it?

The Myth That You Aren't Complete

  Women, from time immemorial, have been told they are not complete without a man in their life. It's in religious scriptures, it's in the fairy tales we are told as little girls, it's the image promoted by the media to little girls and then to teenage girls. It's ingrained in us before we are even born, that a man in our life will take care of us and complete us. This constant message creates a mental pattern in our minds of knights in shining armor and of us relying on others to take on the world for us. It's no different for women in same sex relationships, because it is the mental pattern that affects women. It doesn't matter what sexual persuasion one is. We are raised with the myth that we are not complete without *someone* in our lives.

  We all know of a woman who cannot seem to get through life without a partner of some kind. If they aren't in a relationship, they are talking about being in one, keeping both eyes open for the next opportunity. It's an opportunity because the behavior is not about looking for a partner as a way to help one's growth and development, but about filling a void. This is why there is never any satisfaction in any of the relationships. And this doesn't happen with just single women; married women will expect their spouses to fill the emotional and psychological gaps they feel in their lives—and be expected to do the same for their spouses. But the line "you complete me" from the movie *Jerry McGuire* is just that—a line from the movies. No one completes you, but you. It is a myth created from fairy tales.

  This isn't to put a damper on romance. Finding someone and being in love is a feeling like no other. But being in love is not the same as truly loving someone. Our culture glorifies being in love because it's a time when a person is fun to be around and nothing bothers them. As a society, we are in love with being in love; we love that euphoric feeling and search for it again and again. But when the honeymoon is over and the "being in love" part begins to fade, we don't know what to do next. We want to recapture that feeling, so we continuously go from one relationship to another, each time thinking, "Oh, this might be it!" In reality all we are doing is creating a pattern that isn't about finding love, it's about looking for something to fill an emptiness we feel inside. When we are with someone, we are distracted from the real issues of our personal unhappiness. It is only when we are alone that we have to deal with ourselves and the thoughts that run through our heads.

    With the craze of Facebook, I've reconnected with a number of different people I knew in high school. I initially found it interesting to see what people ended up doing with their lives and who they became. As time went by though, I was taken aback by how many male classmates were married and were not "allowed" to attend any reunion events without their wives; not to mention be friends with any female former classmates! There was a lack of trust among so many of the wives of male friends that I wondered how they even stayed together. The couples "agreed" they could only be friends with people they befriended as a couple. I personally felt this was not only unhealthy, but a sign that they had no faith in their relationship.

    Perhaps I am abnormal (I've been told worse), but I can't understand the jealousy that women feel toward other women who talk to their husbands or partners. I can understand if a former boyfriend or girlfriend from the past suddenly makes contact and every day after, meeting for lunch, etc. There is something to be said for that, but it is unhealthy for a woman to think that her spouse had no life before he met her, likewise for the husband.

    There is a drive in today's culture for everyone to have someone "special" in their life. So much so, that many women feel there is something wrong with them if they don't. A thirty-year-old woman on Facebook was home on a Saturday night and posted, "I'm so lame. Home on a Saturday night." This standard set by society and the media that you aren't normal if you aren't with someone, pushes women into superfluous relationships that don't last. When they don't last, women will look for someone else to prove they are okay. Men do this as well, but women and their need for emotional connection will fret over WHY they can't find love. When they do find it, they don't trust it will last, which leads to agreements like the one mentioned above.

  The belief in the myth that we are not complete without a partner needs to be looked at carefully because it is one of the reasons women find themselves in unhappy relationships and marriages. The saying, "You can't love another until you can love yourself" is not about knowing what "love" feels like. It's about being secure in who you are, accepting the weaknesses you have (but always working toward improving yourself), and trusting yourself. It's about finding all that makes you human, the good, the bad, and the ugly. That is true love. Knowing one's Authentic Self can often lead to a fulfillment that surpasses any other kind of relationship. When we learn to understand our true self and trust our inner knowing, we begin to see life in a very different way because the happiness we are constantly looking for from others is found within ourselves.

The Image and the Reality

Myths play a major part in our lives because so much of what we think is real is based on images we see, whether they are through what we are taught when we are children or through the media. When one begins to pull apart the image and really decipher it, we find that what looks perfect isn't; what we think is the ideal is quite ordinary; and that in reality, things are just the way they are supposed to be. There is no ideal, there is no perfect woman, or perfect way to be. There is a better way, but it depends upon us taking the reins of our lives and moving forward. It also depends upon us being happy with our lives. Happiness comes when we know ourselves and trust in ourselves, not on the images surrounding us that dictate who and how we are supposed to be.

Soon after I quit my job to stay home with my kids, who at the time were one and three years of age, I found myself becoming very unhappy. I didn't want to tell anyone that I found taking care of my kids all day, every day, exhausting and less than mentally stimulating. I worried about what others would think of me as a mother. Now I've come to find that Michelle Obama felt the same way when her girls were little. Close friends of mine, along with my husband, knew I wasn't happy, but it was what was best for our kids. My husband was on the corporate fast track, and despite my own unhappiness, I was happy to watch his career flourish.

Looking back I am very happy with the outcome. But if I had to do it over, I would change a few things. I wish I had been bolder about trying to find a job I could have done from the house. I also would have stayed more in touch with the technological changes that were taking place at that time. But the sacrifices I made then have allowed my husband to start his own company, and my kids to become well-adjusted young adults finding their heart's passion. At the time, however, the story was very different and what made the situation even more difficult for me was another family who lived nearby and seemed like the perfect family.

It had been a year since we had moved into our first house when I started staying home. The perfect family had moved in the same time we did, into the same model house as us, and had three kids—the eldest and youngest were the same age and gender as my kids. If our kids had gotten along, the mom and I probably would have been good friends as she was very likeable and friendly.

I envied the mom and her life. She loved being home with her kids. Her house was always clean and smelled good, she was good looking, had a cute figure despite having had three kids, and always had a lot of energy. Her kids always wore perfect outfits where the colors matched just so, her daughters always had their hair tied up with pretty bows and her son never looked in need of a haircut or of having his nose wiped. I always wondered how she never seemed flustered. Her husband was handsome so they made the perfect looking couple. He had a good job that brought him home at a regular time for dinner, so they would eat dinner, bathe their kids and put them to bed as a couple.

On weekends, they cooked dinner out on their deck that "Brad the Dad" made by himself. When football season started, he brought his large TV out on the deck, had neighbors over, popped the beers, and had a football party. "Perfect Patti" (thank you Tyler Perry) made sure the beers were cold and the hotdogs ready, kept the children at bay by feeding them and allowing them to run her house ragged, and entertained the wives of the husbands who were also kicking back and watching the game. She was the perfect hostess, never looked bothered about anything and on sunny days when her two younger ones were napping, she'd lie on her deck and sunbathe. Everything seemed like it was coming up roses for her and her family.

The reason I envied the mom was because she seemed to have it together. She was never found in dumpy looking clothes. She always had her make-up on. She never seemed to lack energy or want a nap and everything about her felt cozy. She didn't yell at her kids, but quietly walked over and talked to them. Everything she did was "proper." And it was her house where all the kids went because she had the first popsicles of the summer, the first pool out on a hot day, the first pumpkin carving, the first Halloween party, and so on. It was family city at Perfect Patti's house.

My house was a different story. While I was not unhappy with my kids or being a mom, I was unhappy with my life. I had a hard time finding interest in the latest daytime TV or the day after day routine of afternoons spent talking with the other stay-at-home moms. I hated thinking about what to make for dinner and I generally could not wait to go to bed. I was constantly feeling tired and knew it was just boredom. (I think I must have read every book in our little town library.) I felt like I was counting down the hours until I could go back to work and I began to feel envious of my husband's life. I found myself waiting for him to come home to break my own monotony, a very unhealthy thing for anyone to do. Eleanor Roosevelt said, "No one can make you feel inferior without your consent," but Eleanor hadn't met Perfect Patti. As much as I tried to keep myself from feeling inferior and all thumbs, I couldn't get comfortable in my own skin. Perfect Patti was my reminder that my life was far from perfect. And with all my education and all my experience, nothing could stop me from feeling less than joyful.

Four years later, Perfect Patti and Brad the Dad were selling their house. Brad got transferred to another state and Perfect Patti went to work setting up the house to show. She still didn't look bothered by anything. When she talked about moving, she didn't mind that she had to start all over again. She said she looked forward to setting up a new house, making new friends, and so on. Their house was on the market for a year before it finally sold, but Patti didn't mind the constant attention she had to pay to keep the house ready to show nor did she mind handling everything while her husband lived in another state, only coming home on weekends.

About eight months after Perfect Patti and Brad the Dad moved, I was sitting with a neighbor who happened to keep in touch with them. Patti and Brad were getting divorced. I was completely shocked. Brad the Dad had found himself a girlfriend while Perfect Patti was putting their house on the market and getting ready to move. Apparently it wasn't the first time Brad the Dad had been unfaithful and Perfect Patti decided this time she wasn't taking him back. She was done. Brad the Dad moved to Florida to be with his girlfriend, and Perfect Patti (once again) put her new house on the market and took her kids to live with her mom.

When I heard this story, my image of Perfect Patti began to unravel. The truth of the matter, as I later found out, was Perfect Patti was perfect because it was expected of her in her particular faith. She was expected to keep her house clean and comfortable for her spouse. Her children were to be exceptional and perfect, because that was a reflection of her and a reflection of her husband who was, according to their tradition, a channel to God. She was not allowed to complain, but needed to be the good wife and mother. She also believed that if she kept things perfect, her husband wouldn't stray. In the end, I was so shocked that I felt I had awakened from a bad dream. I felt sorry for Patti and for myself.

I felt sorry that Patti suffered from the Mythic Woman syndrome, but I was also sorry that I was so obsessed with the image of Patti, because I was so unhappy with myself. Patti was the image of what I thought was the perfect life. She looked so happy and put together. I kept thinking that if I could just copy a few things that she did, maybe I would *feel* put together. Once I *felt* put together, maybe I would *be* happier. Of course this is all nonsense, but it is no different than what we as women do every day.

We are constantly trying to find some way to keep up with what society tells us is the norm. If it is not society telling us what the norm is, then it is our family. If it is not our family, then it is the stupid little voice in the back of our heads telling us what we need to do to improve our lives. That stupid little voice is the voice of the Mythic Woman. The Mythic Woman is "that" woman. She is the one with the perfect body, the perfect teeth, the perfect personality, who can throw a party at the drop of a hat; has the perfect house; who looks good even on the first or second day of her period; who seems to not have a care in the world; whose hair and make-up always seem just so and who somehow keeps the bar raised while the rest of us keep trying to reach it. But the question is: are we really happy when we strive for perfection? Are women who try to live according to the "rules" of the Mythic Woman, really happy? Or are they grinding their teeth behind their smile and trying to stand up straight while having heart palpitations?

For me personally, I was exhausted from trying to keep everything in order and acting like it didn't make a difference to me. Such behavior is known as denial and it eats you up from the inside out because all the stress from keeping up appearances is internalized. When we accept ourselves for who we are, we have a foundation, a solid foundation, to work from. From there we can build a strong self-esteem and find our own identity. The key is to constantly be aware, because before you know it, the Mythic Woman is whispering in your ear!

Finding Your Sense of Self

Throughout this book, I have talked about the way women will often view themselves based on the standards set by society; how we habitually imbibe the psychological behavior of an oppressed population, though we have the freedom and right to think differently; how we are directed by the media and advertisers to live in a certain way and how they are now focusing their attention on children; how our lack of self-esteem affects our self-determination, and how that, on the whole, affects our ability to discover our Authentic Self.

When we move away from allowing others to influence how we should live our lives, we are left with a blank slate. But figuring out what to do with that blank slate can become intimidating, so I would like to provide some suggestions on how to keep the influence of the Mythic Woman syndrome from haunting your life. These suggestions are not new. There are many different people who recommend such methods and I will try to do them justice by providing their names or the material as a resource. However, like I wrote earlier, finding one's Authentic Self is like learning to ride a bicycle. Unless you get on and continue riding, you'll never feel confident. Truly coming into touch with one's Authentic Self takes time and practice. There will be instances when you question why you are doing what you are doing, or perhaps you will catch yourself reacting or behaving in a particular way. Just wipe your slate clean and start over. Despite making these practices part of my life, I still catch myself getting a tad nervous before meeting people I haven't met before, and my tongue still gets twisted in all sorts of directions when I have to speak to a group of people I don't know. And as you can tell from the previous story, I have allowed the Mythic Woman into my life a few times. (I am sure she is due for another visit soon.)

These practices do work if you are able to keep them in mind throughout your day. Start by picking one to focus on all day and practice it whenever you can. Eventually, they become part of your behavior and when others are having a rough time, you can share your wisdom because you understand it, have practiced it, and can pass it on. It doesn't mean you won't slip. I slip all the time (and I give friends of mine permission to remind me to come back to my senses), but I just keep on trying. It might be a good idea to keep a journal while working through these exercises, because a lot of different thoughts surface that you may want to return to at a later time.

When I started writing out these practices, I wasn't sure which one to start with first. They all interact with one another, so while each has its own impact, they have more impact when they are used in combination with one another—and one almost cannot practice one without practicing another. Interestingly, I had been working with some of these practices and came into contact with a community that lives according to them. Two members of the community, Sanford Danziger and Thomas White, got together and designed a program called the "Totally Responsible Person" or TRP. To know more about the program and how it started, visit **www.trpnet.com.** I have been lucky enough to sit through many sessions of TRP and am always glad to renew my dedication to being a person responsible for my own actions and reactions.

Exercise #1

Silence Within, Silence Without

Silence is always a good place to start because it is something we have so little of in our lives. From the moment we get up in the morning with the buzzing of the alarm clock or radio, until we plop into bed at night to the sound of the TV, we are surrounded by noise. Often, we don't even notice it because we have become so used to it. I once watched an episode of *Brothers and Sisters* where the two Walker sisters want to go to a spa to be quiet, and out of guilt, invite their mother to come. The mother, played by Sally Fields, can't relax to save her life, and needless to say, the daughters don't get the retreat they were hoping for. (Unfortunately, neither do the other clients who attend the spa.) Sally Fields' character represents the women who cannot seem to let go and relax, to the point that no one else can relax around them either. Today, more women talk about finding a place to retreat, either in their own home or at an actual retreat center or spa, because it is being encouraged by society through the media. I was shocked when the word "meditation" actually made it on mainstream TV.

In a society like ours that focuses on having a fit physique, we often don't talk about the need for resting the mind or the psyche. Oprah and some talk show hosts have discussed the benefit of renewing oneself and taking a time-out for relaxation, but it is more than that. Finding the Authentic Self is impossible if the mind is not calm, and there is no better way to calm the mind than through periods of silence. Meditation is a way to achieve this. Many women think this is impossible because of their busy schedules, but all one really needs to do is start out with five minutes a day, every morning, at the same time, in the same quiet area of one's home. Meditation for beginners is nothing more than quieting the mind. The important thing is to allow oneself to be in silence.

I have a dear friend who begged me to teach her meditation. So I began telling her about what it is, the benefits, etc., until she stopped me and said, "No, I want you to teach it to me." I blatantly told her I couldn't. When she asked why, all I could tell her was that she had to practice it in order to learn. I couldn't make her do it. We talked again about a week later. She was having a difficult time with her son, but her voice sounded calm and her demeanor seemed more relaxed as she talked about it. I mentioned the difference in her voice and she laughed saying, "Well, you said I had to do it, so I did. I've been getting up every morning with my cup of coffee and my dog and we sit together on the back porch. I love it. We just sit there in the silence and watch the day begin. Of course I can't really keep my mind still for very long, but I try. And that's all I can do."

Meditation doesn't have to be a big mystery. It's a simple exercise that allows the mind to settle itself. People will say that when they are in their gardens pulling weeds, planting flowers, pruning bushes, or even cleaning up, they find their minds don't think about anything. They consider it their meditation because the mind isn't rambling from one thing to another. Musicians often comment that they find meditation in their art. And while these examples are not the traditional way meditation is done, the result is the same. The mind finds peace from the worries and chaos of everyday life for a few moments.

People who begin meditating in traditional form often find sitting cross-legged on the floor difficult. Zen Masters will tell their students to focus on the discomfort and eventually they won't feel it any longer. I am not as brave as a Zen student despite meditating for over twenty years. But I recommend finding a place that gives you the ability to relax and be comfortable. I don't recommend lying down or you will get sleepy. Start out for five minutes and I can guarantee you that if you continue to practice every day, you will find yourself sitting longer. But more than that, you will notice a change in how you react to situations. You may find you are calmer or more relaxed. This will allow you the mental space to become aware of your thoughts and in turn find the essence of who you are.

If you like movement, then take a walk alone and in silence. Not with your dog or with a neighbor, but alone. If you walk your dog, your thoughts will be about the dog, picking up poop, having a baggy, another dog, someone's yard, and so on. It is amazing where one's mind will go when there is something to distract it. If you walk with a neighbor, you will want to talk, so it is best to just go alone and take time out for your Self.

Exercise #2

Take a Step Back, Don't Give In to Reaction

I have a hard time watching cable news. There is an undertone of edginess and panic in the correspondent's voice that I never heard in someone like Walter Cronkite. On top of all of this, much of the news today is opinionated and no longer objective—telling the news as the news. If I change the channel, most cable shows deal with death, violence, child molestation, animal abuse or domestic problems. It's almost as though there is nothing beautiful in the world. Reality TV, as one person put it, is no different than the freak shows that once came to town which exploited people's disabilities and made them no better than animals at a zoo. Only today, money seems to make up for the exploitation.

Watching the images and hearing the stress and struggle of people just creates more anxiety within us. It creates a mindset that our lives are so much better than those of others, but the fear of "what will happen if it happens to us?" sets in. Fear and anxiety begin to run our lives. I think that is why shows like *American Idol* or *Dancing with the Stars* are such successes. People can truly escape from their own worries. We all have enough problems in our lives and don't really want or need to listen to or see it in our entertainment. However, we still become victims of the anxiety surrounding us, and in turn, we become part of it. We let it into our lives. And as women work on a more emotional level, because the communication area of our brain is larger, we process a lot more of what we see, hear, and experience. So if we surround ourselves with messages that induce fear and anxiety, it becomes part of our reality, whether we know it or not. When it becomes part of our reality, we react to situations and, at times, overreact to them. Women will often get upset with their male partners because men don't react to a situation the same way women do. Men will want to find a solution and be done with the problem. When women react to the situation, they will want to know the details. The more details they have, the more emotion they have about the situation. Many women will often get caught up in the details and tear a situation to pieces, asking advice or consolation from girlfriends, their mothers, and so on, and then complain they are exhausted from talking about it.

I lived with my aunt for six years after my parents died and was taught a wonderful lesson. I had received some news about some situation and immediately said rather loudly, "Oh my God!" and became angry and upset. My aunt calmly looked at me and said, "Why are you reacting like this?" And I began to tell her a number of reasons why I was feeling the way I was, to which she replied, "But you are just wearing yourself out. How do you expect to help anyone if you waste all your energy getting upset or angry?" I never forgot this.

Think of the number of times you have been in a crisis or in an emergency situation. The person we gravitate to most is the one who exudes a calm demeanor. This might be one of the reasons we find strength in some doctors or nurses. Some have the ability to be calm in rather unnerving situations and, in turn, it gives us strength. It might seem odd not to react to a situation or news the way everyone else does, but instead to sit quietly or even not comment for a moment. However, think about what it does to the atmosphere around you. Often, the lack or delay of reaction tends to slow the momentum of a situation down and bring everybody back to their senses.

Finding our Authentic Self requires us to stop reacting and behaving the way we "normally" do, because the energy we spend getting caught up in a situation only pulls us into other people's dramas. When this happens, we are no closer to finding our own identity because we have just taken on another person's problems and emotions. This doesn't mean we don't feel compassion for a person or sympathize with them when they are going through a difficult time, but we don't react blindly to their problem and jump in to match their anger or discomfort. We step back, take a deep breath, and remember there are two sides to every story, if not more.

I'll be perfectly honest; I am better at doing this when my kids are not the ones going through the difficulty. And when my husband and I are disagreeing, I have to watch myself very carefully so I don't say something I will later regret. When in a relationship, we often expect our significant other to understand what we mean when we say something because they are our partner. It is the expectation itself that causes us to react. But the beauty of this exercise is the process it takes you through. When we step back and watch the way we are reacting, we are able to give ourselves time to ask what it is that is causing us to react the way we do. In other words, what is tripping our trigger? It is this process that helps us find our inner sense of Self.

As I had mentioned before, these exercises work together. When we take a few minutes every day to center ourselves, meditate, find our quiet place, rest the mind, we are able to get to that place mentally when an uncomfortable situation arises or when others look to us for strength and guidance. When we are able to get to that place, we react by not reacting. And in turn, we react through choice, not habit. We choose to react or not react a certain way. We become much more conscious of how we are reacting to a situation than just following what everyone else is doing. My aunt used to tell me to "go sit in the audience," which meant that life is very much like a play and we are all characters with different roles. When we choose to sit in the audience, we are able to get a grasp of what each character is doing and where we can best help a situation.

Exercise #3

It's Not about You—Don't Take It Personally

This is a hard one, but it ties directly into not giving in to reaction. Don Miguel Ruiz, a teacher of the Toltec wisdom, writes in his book *The Four Agreements*, four teachings that are simple, yet profound. They are simple, because they are plain common sense. But they are profound because if we could put them into practice regularly (which is the hard part), our lives would be much less complicated. The Four Agreements are: Be impeccable with your word; Don't take anything personally; Don't make assumptions; Always do your best. It is the second agreement "Don't take anything personally" that I want to focus upon. Women often take responsibility for the way others react, because we are people pleasers.

Put very simply, we cannot be responsible for how another person reacts to news we tell them or a mistake we made. But as women we will often take the blame for how another person reacts to something. We feel we have caused their pain. We will try to make the situation better and feel guilty for decades. Why? Really ask yourself this question. Why do we take responsibility for how another person reacts when we have no control over it? The way we react is really a choice. We can choose to blame others, kick, scream, and swear, or we can take a step back and not give in to reaction. Likewise, when someone else is reacting we can choose to make it part of our responsibility or not. When we make it our responsibility, we take the whole situation personally, even when it has nothing to do with us. Likewise when we choose to react by allowing ourselves to feel anger or hurt, we have taken something someone has said personally.

This exercise is very difficult for two reasons. One is that there are situations where pain is going to happen. After twenty years of marriage, suddenly one partner wants a divorce.

It hurts. The partner who wants the divorce has caused the other partner pain and probably a lot of anger. How much pain or anger one is willing to go through is a choice depending on how one chooses to react to the news. In such cases, we take it personally. When we take such news personally, things begin to escalate because we allow the anger and pain to overrule our common sense. If someone doesn't want to be with you, why continue being with them?

The second reason is because it requires discernment. Discernment is the ability to distinguish and select between what is your issue and what is someone else's. We all have issues. There is no one in this world without issues, because there is nothing in this world that does not push our button in some way. And it doesn't have to be negative. Whales and dolphins make me cry. They push my happy button. Watching someone or something that cannot defend itself get picked on or beaten pushes my not-so-happy button. In fact, I get really angry.

Discernment means being aware of where you are emotionally. Young children often don't have discernment because they aren't mature enough to understand what is their issue and what is their parent's. This is why if a parent is having a bad day, children invariably will end up in tears. They don't have the ability to think, "Oh wait, mom or dad is having a bad day and this isn't my problem. What can I do to make them feel better?" I used to warn my kids, "Mommy is upset. This isn't about anything you did." This helped them learn discernment later in life, and like all of us, sometimes they are aware when it's not their issue, and sometimes, they're not.

I know this exercise seems heartless, but when it is used with the other two, it can be used with compassion toward oneself and others. Spending time in silence allows us to become more aware of what we are thinking, discover where our thoughts are originating from, and how to deal with them. It teaches us discernment. If we are disciplined, we force ourselves to look at ourselves without judgment or fear. When we do this for ourselves, we are slowly able to do it for others and we begin to accept and understand people the way they are. We've been judged enough by society, we don't need to be judging ourselves or others. We need to learn to love ourselves, our true selves, so we can love others.

By strengthening our ties to our Authentic Self, we become stronger when someone gives us feedback, positive or negative. We might still feel the sting, but by not giving in to reaction, we are able to listen and be aware of what another is saying. We also are able to find the strength to not allow another's anger or upset to jar us. And in turn, we grow as an individual. It is this growth which brings inner power and control into our lives while maintaining our connection with our Authentic Self.

Exercise #4

Know When it's About You

In Taisha Abelar's book *The Sorcerer's Crossing*, she discusses a method called "recapitulation" which in her story is a technique used by the Toltecs, a group of men and women from Southern Mexico who studied the esoteric side of life, based on ancient teachings. As mentioned previously, Don Miguel Ruiz, author of the *Four Agreements*, is a student of Toltec teaching.

Recapitulation consists of reviewing trauma in one's life, the experience of it, and to understand why we get upset over certain things, why we repeat the same behavior patterns (like surrounding ourselves with people who put us down), or why we fall into the same self-degrading patterns of thinking.

The belief behind this exercise according to the Toltec teachings is that an emotional charge is created within a person when there is a trauma. When a situation in our daily life connects with that charge, the trauma is relived and we become angry or upset without even knowing why. The Toltec weren't off the mark. Our bodies are known to retain memory so any trauma the body or mind experiences, remains with us. However, the Toltec believed that when the charge is created, the life energy we have, becomes depleted. There may be something to this because when we are depressed, we lack energy and everything becomes an effort. The energy we lack may be due to a lack of serotonin, but I think when the heart is not happy, it plays a major role on the body. Recapitulation is an exercise to help one's heart and spirit come back to fullness.

After my parents died, I was a bit of a mess as any seventeen-year-old would be. But it wasn't just my parents' deaths that made me sad, it was everything. Suddenly all the memories of being bullied by the neighborhood kids to being angry with myself for allowing people to take advantage of me came crashing down. I felt cheated by everyone, so by the time I got to India to live with my aunt, I wasn't the most pleasant person to be around. One of the exercises that helped me the most was recapitulation. (Though I did not realize it was called that, it was just something I did.)

Like the previous exercises, recapitulation can only be done in silence and it takes time because it is exhausting. There are memories and emotions that surface and you will question whether they are real or just a dream. In reality, it doesn't matter, because it is obviously a part of you that needs attention. For women, recapitulation is an essential exercise because so much of our energy is given to others throughout our lives. Recapitulation reclaims parts of ourselves from past relationships that did not go well, from the loss of someone we loved, or from the trauma experienced at some point in one's life. It also helps us to see where our weaknesses are in the way we react to situations of the past. By recounting events, memories, and relationships, we are able to find patterns in our behavior and thinking and we begin to know what it is that pushes our buttons, what our issues are, and how to deal with them.

Many books will talk about recapitulation as a way to heal trauma in our life, but I believe that we need to also recapitulate happy events in our life. It is from those memories that we find strength and solace and there needs to be a balance. Recollecting the energy felt at a joyous time, allows us to feel what we felt then and makes the process easier. However, the process of recollecting unpleasant or traumatic events tends to be a lot more difficult to go through. Yet, it is only by going through the whole memory, feeling the energy of the event, and allowing it to finish, that we can finally let it go and find ourselves once more.

Steps to Recapitulation:

Find a quiet place to sit where you feel safe and relaxed. Sometimes, if you enjoy the outdoors, it's nice to sit under a tree or your favorite place in the woods.

When you are comfortable, think of a situation in your life where you would have liked the circumstances to have ended differently; while we cannot change the past, we can change the way we react to its memory. Let the situation, as it happened, play out in your mind. Recollect the event, what was said, the time of the day it happened, where you were, and so on. Allow the memory to surface and run its course. Be aware of what your body is feeling, whether your heart is beating faster, whether you have tension anywhere, and how you are feeling overall.

Once the memory has run its course, it is important to be able to recollect the event without having a reaction, physical, emotional, or mental, to it. The recollection should be just that, a recollection. As you watch the memory, see yourself. How would you have reacted differently? Is the way you reacted then, the way you react now? How can changing the way you react, bring change to your life?

Recapitulating one event does not often happen in a day. It takes time for us not to react to previous events, and some take longer than others. But through recapitulation we are able to see patterns in our behavior and our way of thinking and decide whether they serve us or not. If they don't, we can make the choice to change it.

Exercise #5

Find Out Where You Came From

It is difficult to find your Authentic Self when you don't know who you are or where you came from. Heritage is an important aspect of knowing who you are and may answer why certain things resonate with you, or don't, but more than heritage, it is beneficial for everyone to understand patterns in their family. The patterns of your family, patterns of either health or behavior, allow you to see and answer questions about yourself, thus bringing you one step closer to your Authentic Self.

As a counselor-in-training, one of the most interesting assignments I was given was creating a genogram. (Go to www.genogram.com.) A genogram is a diagram you design of generations of your family, along with dates of when they were born, who they married, how many kids they had or didn't have, and so on. For a class I took in counseling, we were required to draw a genogram to analyze repetitive behavior patterns, i.e., marrying young, alcoholism, drug abuse, divorce. It also helps identify health patterns in the family like cancer or diabetes and even depression, which can follow one generation after another. While it sounds like a rather emotionally convoluted exercise, it is actually very eye-opening. Like the exercise in stepping back and not giving into reaction, genograms allow us to see patterns on paper that we might follow because our family members followed them.

The beauty of knowing where you came from gives you the ability to embrace or discard certain patterns that don't resonate with you. Granted, this is difficult when the pattern is genetic or biological and somewhat out of our control. But a genogram also shows us that we don't have to believe the myth that our families believe or hold as their truth. We don't have to follow their patterns of behavior. We can create our own. Once we see it in front of us, we can make the choice to act differently, and in turn move toward living authentically and from our true sense of Self.

Exercise #6

Write Your Story

When you feel comfortable enough, write your story. We all have one. Just take a step back and look at your life. There's your story. You don't have to share it with anyone, or even let anyone know you are writing it. Just write. Even if your spelling is bad, or you don't write well, don't worry about it. Write your story for you. It is one of the best ways for women, especially, to see the impact our culture has made on them.

Starting is a lot easier if you don't think about it. Write about your relationships with your parents, your siblings, people who made an impact on your life, the lessons you learned from them, and the events that changed your life. It is sort of like recapitulating on paper and it is very moving, because you will have the chance to see *you* through *your* eyes. You realize you are a person who needs to be cared for just like the friends you care about. When I was a kid, I remember having the realization that only I could see through my eyes and I wondered if everyone saw what I did. But we don't. While many young girls and women share similar life experiences, we don't necessarily feel those experiences in the same way no matter how personal they are. So many of the things we later experience in life originate because we are women. Our bodies are a living library and can tell an incredible story.

The other wonderful thing about writing your life story is that it will keep changing. Incidents recollected from childhood may end up becoming clearer once put on paper. In turn, once we see it on paper and are able to read how we saw something, we are able to process things, reflect on them, and eventually let them go. As I try as much as possible to walk my own talk, I wrote my story as part of this book. It is just a snippet of my life, but the process was cathartic. What I realized most about writing my own story was that my story is my interpretation, seen through my eyes. Yet there are a number of versions of the same story because of the number of people I interacted with. They could tell you the same story but from their point of view. There are two, sometimes three or more, sides to a story and we need to give people the benefit of the doubt when they see something differently than we do. We aren't seeing things through their eyes. It doesn't necessarily mean we have to agree with it, it just means we need to allow them their place in the story, interpreted through their eyes.

Exercise #7

Find Your Voice

As we come more into touch with our Authentic Self, it's important to move out of our comfort zone, and voice our opinions and speak up when we need to, even when it is for something that may make us unpopular. This might seem like something one is told in second grade, but women tend to not say anything when an injustice is being done to them. It happens in schools and colleges, in work environments, and even when you think you are surrounded by those who "have your back."

I have to admit, I am still working on this exercise and this book is part of that process. It has been said that women are better listeners than men, but despite our communication centers being larger in our brains, we have a difficult time expressing ourselves. Communication is about talking *and* listening. Deborah Tannen writes in her book *You Just Don't Understand* that men and women use talking for different reasons. She says women communicate to build relationships (rapport) while men communicate to get the facts (report) and maintain order in their social world. This is considered sexist by some and on the mark by others. But the difference in communication between men and women, and the trials it undergoes, may be lessened if we all learned to how to truly communicate with one another.

With regard to women, if we do communicate to build relationships, we cheat ourselves by not communicating when we need to. We tend to shy away from confrontation and would rather be peacemakers. It's part of our upbringing under the Mythic Woman culture. We don't want to ruffle feathers. But sometimes we need to step out of our comfort zone and express that which we don't agree with. We don't have to be rude or confrontational in doing so, or even apologetic. We can be direct and concise which will make people take what we say seriously.

By working with the above exercises, we move away from the expectations of society and everyone around us and find our inner strength to stand up for issues that matter to us. We realize that we are the only ones given the right to live our life. It doesn't belong to anyone else but us, and if we keep allowing others to make decisions for us or assume their opinion matches ours, we are doing ourselves an injustice. Our voices are a tool to be able to express ourselves and there is no reason, other than fear, for us not to. So speak up, even if your voice quivers!

Creating a New Culture

Changing a culture is no different than creating one. It starts with individuals. Women have slowly been changing the culture that surrounds them and changing the way they live their lives. We've changed the way we are viewed in relationships with our significant others, we've fought for equal rights, (we've even taken on the Church!), we've created the women's movement. We've pushed for better legislation that protects us from losing our jobs when on maternity leave or when needing to take care of a family member. The culture we live in now is different than what women lived in fifty years ago. But we still have a long way to go. We still deal with sexual discrimination in the workplace, unspoken sexism in our society, and the innate inability to step out of the patterns that for so long have kept us from finding our Authentic Self.

In an effort to empower ourselves, various modes of what empowerment means have been created. During the women's movement of the 1970s, some women felt it necessary to do away with femininity, thus doing away with anything that had to do with marriage, family, or other domestic roles women have traditionally played in society. Sadly, this was yet another aspect that got a lot of media attention, though it was only one subsection of the women's movement. And while there are women who find empowerment in not marrying or having a family, they are a small population compared to the number of women, lesbian or straight, who find partners and choose to start a family.

Another form of empowerment among female teens is the idolization of their bodies. But as mentioned before, this form of empowerment was not created by women but the media, which unfortunately is still dominated by patriarchal patterns of thinking. And still another culture, not mentioned before, made popular by male hip hop and rap artists, is where the term "bitch" and "ho" are used to evoke power for women. These artists claim that by "taking back the word" like the GLBT (Gay, Lesbian, Bisexual, and Transgender) Movement did, we give it a different connotation. However, in this regard, and the ones before it, I don't believe that is true. Women did not take back the words of "bitch" and "whore"; men did, and it is still used in a derogatory fashion toward females. I cringe when a girl calls another girl "her bitch." The terms are not empowering, they depict ownership, domination, and immense cruelty.

    To change a culture, we need to change the language we use, the way we think, the way we view ourselves, and the way we relate as women with one another. Most importantly, WOMEN need to do this for WOMEN. And not just for White women or Black women or Hispanic or Chinese women, just women. Because no matter where you come from or what your walk in life has been, living authentically goes beyond race, religion, sexual orientation, or any other category. Despite the many categories we can use to find difference among us, there are experiences that women have in common. Can we use that as a common ground to put aside our differences and create a culture that serves us all? Can we use the power we create by coming together to form a community whose goal is to make the world better not only for ourselves, but for all women? Can we help each other by advocating for one another, and help each other find the strength to speak up and have our concerns and issues taken seriously? In essence, can we learn from one another?

    Gloria Steinem, in a 2006 interview with Marianne Schnall from *Femininist.com* said, "If I could have one structural wish for the women's movement, it would be that we have a kind of Alcoholics Anonymous group structure all over the world, so that wherever you go in a different village or town you can find the feminist equivalent of an AA group to go to once a week and to get some support, and some help with seeing the politics of what's happening to us." This would definitely be one way to reconnect women to each other and to their own sense of self, breaking the myth that we need to look outside of ourselves to a patriarchal society to find out who we are.

It may seem stereotypical to say, but women are about connecting and learning from one another and like some anthropologists have claimed, it may have to do with our survival instincts from centuries ago. There is a resiliency we gain from being with other women who support us and care for us unconditionally, and for some of us, we find that in our female friends more than we do in our own biological family members. And there is nothing wrong with that. What is important is to have that support and the ability to call on that support without question. Would you think twice about calling a girlfriend at three in the morning? And as the girlfriend being called, would you answer the call without question? As you ask yourselves these questions, think of what your immediate thought was. Did you start out, "Well, yeah, if she . . ." *Without question*, meaning without *conditions*.

This hypothetical situation might seem silly, but think about how many times we hesitate to ask for help, or worse, we hesitate to offer help. We are so worried about bothering our friends. Part of the patriarchal perspective is that we need to take care of ourselves, deal with our own situations, manage our own difficulties, not worry about others, and not ask for help. It's a very individualistic viewpoint, one that can be very detrimental to our well-being, especially for women. Most people would agree that we learn more about ourselves by being with others than we do on our own. This is why communities where everyone works for the good of the whole, thrive and prosper compared to those that don't; likewise for organizations and companies. But it takes work and it takes connection.

By knowing ourselves and changing our personal culture, we are able to slowly focus on changing societal culture which for so long has been a patriarchal society, where things are viewed from a male perspective. And we can continue to exist this way, but we are existing from only one perspective, one that has been created for us. We're not truly living. This doesn't mean that everything created by men or anything to do with men is horrible. Patriarchy is a system, and as I mentioned before, it is the system that needs to change. Interestingly, the economic downfall may be the initiation of a change in that system as there are more women in the workforce than men for the first time in US history.

A major factor that holds us back from living our lives authentically, and creating a difference in how we are viewed, is fear. As individuals we fear what will happen if we don't follow the pattern and expectations that society sets for us, and that makes life very ambiguous. There are ways out of this perception, but like anything else it takes work on an individual basis first. It also takes time, because as mentioned in the beginning of this book, to be truly comfortable with ourselves is a process. It starts with baby steps and most of the time when the going gets rough we find a reason to quit. Think of the number of times you've wanted to lose or gain weight or just get into better physical shape. We keep putting it off because of something—our work, our kids, a family crisis, the weather, or writing a book! We've all done it at some point in our lives. And then there are some who have this epiphany about never putting off until tomorrow what can be done today and making all the rest of us jealous (or crazy).

It is obvious from the number of stories that surface about females, whether it is about young girls starving themselves, young college women participating in behavior that is not only risky but possibly dangerous, and women in general suffering from depression and low self-esteem, that there is a problem. At first I would read some of the stories and think "there goes the media again, creating drama" because there are rarely any positive stories about females. We're always suffering from some crisis. But when I took a closer look and talked to other women, I realized it wasn't just the media that was *presenting* the crisis; it was that women *are* in crisis. And like everything else about women, it is a quiet crisis. No different from the 1950's woman who would lock herself in the bathroom, muffle her screams with a towel, wipe her tears, reapply her makeup, and come out as though the world was wonderful. Yet, today that woman expects more from herself or does more—each time trying to reach the bar that society raises. It's only when we ignore the standards set and follow our own promptings that we will find an inner peace.

While I have my own visions of what I would love to see in the lives of other women, I know that all I can do is keep "doing" and, in turn, hope that whatever inspiration is found in the pages of this book, you, the reader, in turn inspire another woman. And somehow, like the ripples in a pond, more women find their Authentic Self and lay to rest the Mythic Woman.

I was talking to a friend about this closing chapter and she said, "Yes, and we need to trust the process. After all, isn't it the same experience at a different degree?" In other words, each time we find inspiration from others, the effect might be very small at one time and deeper the next, depending on what we need to hear and where we are in our lives. But it is truly a matter of trusting the process, following that inspiration to wherever it may take you, and learning from the experience.

This is probably the most difficult chapter to write because the slate is blank. Women from the past, our suffragette sisters, have marked the path, our mothers and grandmothers from the women's movement laid the earth, and while there are young women who have no hesitation about walking down the road, there are more who are not sure which direction to take.

The signs are confusing, the road seems too long and vast, and there is always something "more important" to do. But in the end, what could be more important than listening to your inner voice, finding your Authentic Self and becoming the person you truly want to be?

My Story

I feel sometimes that in order to get a person to move out of their comfort zone, the universe throws them whammies. In my life things snowballed. It started with one event and then just kept going. Perhaps it does that for all of us. But for me there was a specific time when things kind of kept on rolling and one thing after another happened. Looking back, I realize these were all stepping stones. Each one needed to be touched, stepped upon firmly. Each stone was an experience and while there were some experiences I would have rather not gone through, I believe they were all essential to get me to where I am today.

When I was younger, I remember friends saying I should write a book about my life. I never thought I would ever have anything to say that others hadn't already thought about. Then one day another friend told me that it didn't matter if the book was going to be read by one person or a million, just write. Write from the heart. Write what you feel needs to be said and leave it up to the universe as to whether anyone else needs to read it. Just write.

I can only write from what I know and what I have experienced as a woman, a mother, a sister, an aunt, a great-aunt, and as my Self: who I am after all the roles are played and put aside. It took me a while to find solace in myself, in my own beliefs, in my own skin; not caring whether others agreed with me or not. After talking to a number of other women, I realized that perhaps there was something I could say that others needed to hear. It wasn't anything new, but it was my experience and perhaps that added a difference to it.

I am sure there were other incidents that happened before the snowball started, but the initial incident that began the avalanche was my mother dying when I was sixteen, because of complications due to alcoholism. According to my mom, when she was twelve, she found her father shortly after he had committed suicide. My mother said he shot himself in the head, but the death certificate said it was a gunshot wound to the chest. As she had a close relationship with her father and couldn't understand why he would do such a thing, she struggled with feelings of inadequacy and victimization. She married her high school sweetheart, but the marriage ended two years later as her first husband was an alcoholic. According to my dad, when he met my mom, she was sleeping on the floor of her mother's apartment and to avoid being home, she would work double shifts at the hospital.

Two weeks after my mom died, my father found out he had terminal throat cancer. He died eight months later. After he was diagnosed, he decided to hand his case over to Fermi Lab in Batavia, Illinois. They were experimenting with something called neutron therapy at the time, a government funded project. My father had to sign a waiver stating that he could lose his hair, his sight, his ability to eat, and possibly his life. It didn't really matter to him because he was a thoracic surgeon and knew that throat cancer at that time was a death sentence. It was either neutron therapy or to have his voice box and tongue removed and eat through a tube in his stomach. I remember when he returned home after the diagnosis, he was more concerned about whether he would be able to continue to practice medicine than whether he would die. I think it was this statement that made me believe he would survive the cancer. He chose the radiation and survived the therapy with third degree burns on his neck that eventually healed. However, the arteries in his neck and chest were weakened and after a few weeks of internal bleeding, he hemorrhaged and died. My aunt, his elder sister, and my great aunt, my grandfather's sister, were with him when he took his last breath.

I didn't see either of my parents after they died. There was no closure to the year of losing both of them. The morning of the day my mother died, I went to the hospital to visit her. She was in the ICU and was being given oxygen. The only thing I remember was the look in her eyes and her inability to breathe. She looked incredibly scared. The bed was so high I couldn't kiss her goodbye when it was time to leave. The hospital staff handed me a plastic bag that contained my mom's clothes and her belongings. I was either too stupid or too naïve to understand what was going on. I didn't realize the hospital packed up everything for you when they knew your loved one was going to die. I thought they wanted me to do her laundry. My father didn't explain anything to me, because I was an emotional teen at the time and he wasn't sure how I would react.

After my mother died in July, my father started a six week therapy course in September. It finished at the end of October. I remember seeing him once while the sessions were going on and almost didn't recognize him. He was half the size he normally was and looked exhausted. In December, he left for India. It must have been arranged with his sister who came to the US from India for a lecture tour right after my mom died and cancelled everything to care for my father. At the time, my aunt had just been elected international president of the Theosophical Society. She traveled around the world, gave talks about self-study, and crossed paths with extraordinary thinkers and public figures. Despite her position at the time, she never thought twice about stepping in to help my brother, sister, and me when our world was falling apart.

My father died on St. Patrick's Day in 1982. It was my junior year in high school. I remember borrowing a green sweater from my girlfriend to wear to school, but, of course, I never made it to school the next day or the next, or the next. My brother came home one day from work and told me I needed to go back to school. He said it was important to try to get back to a normal life. But none of our lives were normal. And I remember questioning what normal was after everything I had been through. I fell into a depression and began a downward spiral into a life of harm to myself. It's amazing how differently we all react to situations, teenagers especially. In a world where one doesn't feel wanted, a person will do anything to get attention, and that's what I did.

The month after my father died, my aunt came to the US to talk to us about his death. She went into detail about what happened days before he died, what happened the night he died, and how his face became so serene after he took his last breath that it seemed like he was sleeping. She talked about how death was just another part of life and not to fear it, but to accept it. Of course while she was saying all this, I was sobbing. I couldn't think about my father without crying. Every time someone recollected something that happened, I was overwhelmed with sorrow. At the time, I don't ever remember feeling such despair. His death was finality for my own life. I wasn't sure how I was going to move forward. I used to think people exaggerated when they spoke of someone being their pillar of strength, but my father was that for me. Everything always seemed like it would all be okay because he was there.

My aunt was very aware of how fragile I had become. I had just turned seventeen, lost two people whom I was very close to, and I knew nothing about the world. I knew how to take care of a house, my sister who was disabled from cerebral palsy, and I could run a checking account. But I lived in a vacuum. My mother had been my role model and while she was incredibly kind and selfless toward her children, she constantly reinforced that I didn't need brains because I would get by on my good looks. My parents' nickname for me was "cute little thing" and I was encouraged to be the entertainer. It would have been fine if the world saw me that way, but it didn't. In the end, it did more harm than good.

In an effort to put some control back in my life, my aunt kept encouraging me to visit India. I didn't know how to say no, so I kept saying "maybe." The year before I finally left was awful. It was almost as though the universe wanted to steer me in a direction I didn't want to take, so it made my life hell. My brother and his wife had moved into the home my parents had owned. I think the house was mortgaged to the gills so my brother took over the payments. The stress of managing the bills, their new baby (their daughter was born in October while my father was having his therapy), and me wrecked havoc over the household. My brother and I are five years apart, so we were constantly fighting as he tried to be a parent and brother. As I couldn't get a full-time job, I was always babysitting my niece to the point that people thought she was mine. I had no skills or education to speak of, was financially on my own, and was emotionally and mentally imbalanced due to the sudden change in my life.

Knowing nothing about the world, I had no idea that there were organizations that could help me or that would pay for my education because I was orphaned. The sound of the word orphan made me angry, because it brought home the fact that I was truly parentless. The mom of one of my classmates offered to have me come live with them because she felt I needed a home that was parented. I remember getting angry when my classmate said something to me about it. I have always regretted that. Her mom was doing exactly what I would do right now if such a thing happened to a friend of one of my kids. But I was angry about everything. I was angry that my parents were not there to take care of me, that I was learning life the hard way, that I wasn't smart enough to go to college, that I wasn't beautiful, that I wasn't rich, that I didn't feel confident in my life, that I wasn't somebody's somebody . . . the list went on and on.

Meanwhile, my aunt kept sending me letters asking me to come to India. I had been to India once before with my father when I was twelve and loved being there. People were kind, the place where we stayed was beautiful, and I fell in love with my Indian family. I had never met them before, but it felt as though we had all known each other for years. Most of my family members were vegetarians and after a week of not eating meat, my body started craving it. It was a very strange sensation. I kept chewing gum to get rid of the craving. I had wanted to be a vegetarian when I was seven after figuring out where meat came from, but my mother wouldn't allow it. I protested, but was made to eat what she cooked. Despite her being married to an Indian, my mother never learned Indian cooking and she didn't enjoy eating it. I wish my dad was alive today so I could cook him a good South Indian meal.

My family in India was not normal either, but not in the dysfunctional sense of the word. Apparently we didn't follow the normal Hindu customs or rituals, except for the basic ones of cleanliness toward food, one's body, and one's surroundings. However, I didn't realize how outside of the box my family was until I finally lived there. When I was twelve I just happily enjoyed meeting all my new aunts, uncles, and cousins (and I had a lot of them). My father had quite a time trying to explain to me how everyone was related. Suffice to say, I had a lot of uncles, aunts, and cousins. But I was welcomed with open arms and wrote home to my mom that I didn't miss her at all. My brother later told me that was the worst thing I could have said. I meant that she didn't need to worry about me—she took it a different way.

My grandfather had already passed away by the time I first went to India. He was the eldest of eight children and had three brothers and four sisters. All of them were remarkable in their own way. One of the brothers married a woman from Detroit, Michigan. Her name was Norma and I connected with her right away when I met her. She was very outgoing, rode a bicycle, wore a sari and was very funny. I adored my other great aunts, but they were very quiet, moved slowly, and didn't talk very much. I wasn't used to such a reserved way of being, but reveled in it after maturing and living in India. But during that particular visit, Norma stole my heart. She invited my father and me to lunch, served us *papad*, and told me it was a huge potato chip so I would eat it. She told me funny stories about growing up on a farm in Michigan and was able to relate to me at my level. She was so different from my great uncle who was soft-spoken and didn't talk much. But he loved Norma passionately and was incredibly affectionate to her. I wish I had gotten to witness more of their relationship.

It was Norma who got the ball rolling of getting me to India after my dad passed away. She was coming to the US to have eye surgery and needed an escort back. (She didn't really, but this is how she hooked me into going to India.) Would I travel back with her? I went and got my passport and then went to the Indian Consulate and got my visa. My aunt kept telling me to get an entry visa which was good for a year and I remember thinking I would have to stay for a whole year and felt very hesitant. Despite having loved it six years earlier, I intended this time to visit for six months and go back to the US. I was dating a boy I liked. He was kind, didn't drink a lot (I had been dating alcoholics and drug users), and he kept talking about a future for us. And I didn't really think I had any other choice other than marriage because isn't that what every girl dreams of?

Norma and I arrived in India in the wee hours of September 23, 1983. When she was alive, we always remembered the date and celebrated in a small way. Even today, I always remember the date in honor of her. As we were driving through the campus where I would live for the next six years, I remember the moon being bright, but I could be mistaken. The autumn equinox had just passed and Norma said it was a good time for a new beginning. We had left on September 21 and arrived on the 23rd. What I do remember very clearly was that my great uncle Yagna, Norma's husband and my grandfather's younger brother, was sitting at his desk waiting for his bride to come home. His hearing was almost gone by that time and Norma had to shout or mime things for him to understand. What was unmistakable was the sheer joy in his eyes when she walked through the door. He stood up slowly, smiled such a subtle little smile and said "Norma!" very softly. Norma didn't have to say anything, she just allowed herself to be circled in his arms. Uncle Yagna was in his eighties by this time and Norma was in her seventies. They had been married for over thirty years, but one would have never known.

My first few weeks in India were, to say the least, difficult. Despite my cousin, who was twenty years older than I, keeping me company and Norma being just across the way, I don't think anyone was really sure what to do with me. Only later did I find out from my cousin that she was sort of left in charge of me. It was a pretty difficult task. I was a typical American eighteen year-old. My life consisted of my boyfriend and what I looked like. I remember feeling so jealous of my cousin because everything she wore looked beautiful on her. She was taller than me with a thin physique and moved so gracefully.

I had been athletic most of my eighteen years and had always been skinny as a kid. Even though I was short, I had thin muscular legs. However, in my state of depression, I stopped running and exercising so all my muscle turned into fat. By the time I went to India, I looked like Bulk Hogan to say the least. It didn't help that I had stopped eating regular meals and began periods of binging. I proudly told everyone that I was a vegetarian, even though all I ate were peanut butter sandwiches on white bread.

After getting to India, I met a man not much older than myself who kept telling me that I needed to exercise. I found India too hot to do any kind of running. I tried playing tennis once, but felt so heavy and clumsy (and HOT), that I tired quickly. Everyone kept saying I was just weak and needed to gain stamina. I wasn't sure what was wrong with me. Looking back now I know I was just depressed. I had no friends, no one to talk to, was in a foreign country, had nothing to do, and was adjusting to the food, the culture, the heat, the customs, the dirt, and the poverty. On top of all of this, I didn't feel like me. I didn't know who "me" was, but I knew that the girl my parents raised died after they died. Once upon a time, I loved nature and could easily spend time alone in the woods writing poetry, but here I was living on a wooded 250 acre campus, and feared wandering out alone. I felt grumpy and useless as I didn't know what to do with myself. My aunt was busy with work and visitors and I couldn't participate in any of the conversations because I didn't know what they were talking about. I had little knowledge of what was happening in the world. Every morning my aunt would read the newspaper before going to work and discuss an item she thought would pique my interest, but it didn't. My mind was completely dull. All I wanted to do was go back to the US.

About three months after being in India, I made friends with some of the other kids who lived on campus. I remember being surprised they spoke English, knew Western music, and wore Western clothing. What I didn't realize was how much smarter they all were and how their eagerness to understand the world would wear off on me. While they didn't know where each state was in reference to another, they knew the east coast, west coast, northern, and southern sections of the US and would always ask what coast a state was near. I neither knew the names of the states in India nor where they were. I became friends with a boy who shared the same name as my grandfather because my grandfather was loved and honored by his family. He was one of my lifelines until I was able to establish my own roots in a country I had a lot to learn about.

    Another lifeline I found was my family and its history. The more I discovered about the strength and courage of every member in my family, the more I realized that I carried that strength and courage in my own DNA. I just needed to find it within me. What helped the most was living with two very strong, intelligent women, my aunt and great aunt, who had decided to follow their dreams and not to marry just because society (Indian society, mind you!) expected it. My great aunt Sivakamu, one of my grandfather's younger sisters, was married, but realized she wanted to forfeit her marriage and instead dedicate her life to medicine. This was considered scandalous during her time in India and to make matters worse, my grandfather supported her decision. My great grandfather had died leaving my grandfather, the eldest son, to manage the family affairs and be the spokesperson for the family.

    My grandfather was a man of his own mind and didn't pay much attention to what others thought. He was very much for the equal rights of women long before it was fashionable to say so, and while he didn't care what others thought, he was never boastful, proud, or arrogant. On the other hand, he was incredibly gentle and loving in his demeanor, never spoke a harsh word, was well-read, and articulate. If there is anyone I epitomize, it's my grandfather. The few times I met him as a child, I always felt as though I was in the presence of a holy person. I later found out that I wasn't the only one who felt this.

    I believe part of what made my grandfather such a peaceful individual was his ability to not get caught up in the nonsense of the everyday world. He was a very good administrator and despite being incredibly busy as international president of the Theosophical Society, a position he held for twenty years, the pressures he faced never ruffled him. There is a story that he was in the Philippines and went to visit the president of the country. The president kept him waiting for two hours (or perhaps longer). My grandfather, it is said, did not seem bothered. What would annoy most people, did nothing to him. He quietly read a book and waited patiently. Chances are he probably enjoyed the break. But his idea of what was important was outside the ordinary realm. The Buddhists have a line that states, "React to neither praise nor blame," which means that neither one holds any importance. One day everyone will love you and tell you how wonderful you are. The next day everyone will be angry and tell you how stupid you are. Which is the truth? Neither.

As the head of an Indian household, my grandfather was expected to keep a certain standard, but because he didn't believe in the standard, he did what he believed was right. So when my great aunt decided she no longer wanted to be married and she had cleared everything with her husband, my grandfather went and brought her back home. Apparently, there was an outcry by the community and by the more orthodox members of our family. But my grandfather paid no heed and never regretted his decision. My great aunt Sivakamu went on to become an Ob-Gyn and assisted in the birth of the children for the Maharani of Bikaner in Rajasthan. She also started an orphanage for abused and neglected children, adopted two little girls from the orphanage and raised them herself, initiated a program to neuter the male dogs in her town to stop the overpopulation of puppies, and paid for her ex-husband's children's college education. She lived to the lovely age of ninety-four.

While my aunt, my father's sister, is extraordinary in her own way, her temperament is very different than my grandfather's or any of his brothers and sisters. My great aunt

Norma once told me the story of how, when she was close to thirty, she met my aunt who was just fourteen. She said that my aunt had such presence of intention, precision, and grace that it made Norma feel like she was all thumbs. She said it was the oddest thing to feel intimidated by a fourteen-year-old, but there she was. My aunt has a very direct temperament which often leaves one speechless. It is never meant to be rude or imprudent, but just the way she is. While living with her, she kept a very rigid household. Breakfast was at six-thirty, lunch at eleven-thirty, and dinner at six-thirty. She stuck to this schedule as much as possible, out of concern for the servants who ran the house, and who had families and other things they would like to do.

    I was not used to the strict tone of voice, the set hours, or the constant need to be aware of what I was doing. There would be nights of feeling completely lost, especially if my cousin had left and gone back home. But because I felt uncomfortable with my environment, I spent a lot of time journaling, like I used to, and reading. I slowly found my mind opening to other worlds, values, a different culture, and a new way of looking at myself. The constant vigilance of what I said, how I said something, how I ate my food, how I wore my hair, and so on, made me mindful of everything I did. I know it sounds like badgering, but many ancient teachings talk about teachers who are hard on their students so they become better people than their teachers.

    In the first six months after I had arrived, there was a discussion with my family about my name. When I was born I was given the name Susan Adrienne. It never seemed to fit me. I was constantly changing it from Susan to Suzan to Susie to Suzi to Addy to Adrienne and nothing ever felt right. Sometimes our name can be like an item of clothing that just doesn't fit well. We fiddle with it and keep adjusting it, but it never lies against our skin correctly. Eventually the best thing to do is to just discard it. When I got to India, I think I told Norma, and then my cousin, that I didn't feel like my name ever fit me. The news got back to my aunt that I wanted to change my name and we began discussing the meanings of names. It didn't seem to be an issue with any of my family members that I wanted to change my name. In fact it seemed almost normal, as though it was part of the change I was going through.

While we were working on finding me a name that was suitable, Ramchandra Gandhi came and had dinner with us. He was a professor of philosophy at the University of Hyderabad as well as Professor of South Asian and Comparative Philosophy at the California Institute of Integral Studies. (And yes, he was related to Mahatma Gandhi. He was one of his grandsons.) The discussion about my name became the topic at the dinner table and Professor Gandhi said that one of his favorite names was Ananya—translated as "an" meaning "no," and "anya" meaning "other." He went on to emphasize that the meaning had nothing to do with being special such as when one says "there is no other like it." It means there is no separation, everything is one, there is no "other" because everything is part of the unity. Nothing is more special or better than anything else. The uniqueness lies in the commonality or unity of it all.

I remember that evening very clearly because it was the night I was named. I didn't choose it. It was chosen for me by everyone at the table. After Professor Gandhi talked about the meaning of the name, everyone looked at me and said "Ah, Ananya." That night when my cousin and I were turning in for the night, she very quietly said, "Goodnight, Ananya."

With my move to India, the new friendships I had made, and the changing of my name, something shifted within me. As an international figure, my aunt traveled a lot, so I was left with my great aunt Sivakamu who was already quite elderly. I found myself falling in love with this aunt as well and didn't mind being alone with her. She would tell me stories about her life and our family that I wish I had written down. And because I had no pressure to be anywhere, I would practice the discipline of being aware of myself, my thoughts, and so on, while looking after this incredible woman who was as beautiful in her eighty years as she was when she was a young woman.

But despite the changes I had gone through, the adjusting I had done, and the new life I began to lead, I still had remnants of the anxiety I used to feel as a child. There was still a tension that I would hold in between my eyes—which has come back to haunt me as I still carry my tension there—and in parts of my face. My lack of confidence was prevalent in my eyes, but was slowly melting away. One morning as I sat meditating (something else I had started doing), I suddenly asked myself why I carried all my hardships from the past with me. What good did they do? What purpose did they serve in my life? I realized, truly realized, for the first time in my life what it was like to let go. I let go of my anger, frustrations, sadness, my attachment to what others thought; I just let go and wiped the slate of my life clean.

I remember it was hot that morning and I was sitting cross-legged on the floor of my room, facing a small altar of things special to me. I began sweating despite having the fan running full blast, but decided I was going to ignore my discomfort and plod away. I don't remember anything spectacular happening when this experience took place. I just remember seeing a little chalk board in my mind and hearing that life is like a blank slate and we have the choice to keep it filled with scribbles or to wipe it clean. The vision was so visceral that I was enveloped in it. Nothing existed for those few seconds except the bliss of truly understanding that my life was self-determining. I had the choice, I had the control, and for once in my young years, I had come into touch with who "I" truly was.

My description of this experience is insipid compared to the actual event and the impact it made on the rest of my life. Letting go and wiping the slate clean was like an emotional, mental, psychological, spiritual wash. I don't feel I lost any part of who I am, but, on the contrary, have come more into touch with my true Self. What were once painful images of the past and from my childhood, no longer hold any attachment to me. Yes, there are times I wish my parents were physically here, but the deep sorrow dissipated and the images are nothing more than leaves blowing across a landscape.

My aunt was out of town when I had my "wiping the slate clean" experience, so when she returned, I went outside to greet her. She smiled at me and said, "There is a difference in your face." I didn't need to say anything to her. Whatever I was experiencing within me was showing on the outside as well. Once she was settled in from her trip, I told her what had happened. She did not react to the incident, but quietly said, "Sometimes our environment allows these things to happen." And it was very true. My aunt had no radio or TV. Even if she did at the time, there would have been little to watch as it was expensive to have constant broadcasting in those days. Today, things have changed tremendously and being in India can sometimes feel like you are in the US.

Aside from no media distractions, I was surrounded by nature. I lived right on the Bay of Bengal and was a stone's throw from the beach. Every evening was spent walking on the beach, watching the sunset on one side and the moonrise on the other. At that time, people complained about the filth on the beach, but it was nothing compared to what it is today. Long ago, the Adyar beach had seen many full moon picnics and late night swims, just as it is still witness to many early morning walkers and yoga students who come to greet the morning sun. This was my life for six years and I didn't realize how precious it was until my slate wiping experience.

Relaxing in my own skin allowed me to see the beauty that surrounded me. I stopped getting angry about things and let things go because it didn't matter anymore. At the same time I became almost militant about kindness toward animals, plants, and the environment. It bothered me to watch things suffer. I wanted to do things to relieve the suffering of all creatures, so became involved in animal welfare and environmental causes.

Despite years of feeling intellectually inadequate and thinking I wasn't smart enough to go to college, settling in my own skin gave me the confidence to do things I never thought I would. I completed my Bachelor's degree in Sociology in India and after coming back to the US, acquired my Masters degree in public administration, specializing in non-profit organizations. It didn't dawn on me that it was an accomplishment until my brother mentioned that out of the three of us (my brother, sister, and I), I was thought to be the one who would not go to college. It was considered ironic, because neither my mom nor my dad expected me to do well academically. I was considered the "cute" one of the family. Intellectual pursuits were an expectation of my brother.

So this is my story. And I recommend you write yours. For one thing, it gives a person the ability to actually look at their life on paper. The ability to see what one has gone through, where one's strengths lie, the ups and downs of life, and the joy of reading who one is, is just one way of coming back to the essence of oneself. You don't have to share it with anyone (or you can go out on a limb and publish it in a book for the world to see.)

Our deepest fear is not that we are inadequate. Our deepest fear is that we are powerful beyond measure. It is our light, not our darkness, that most frightens us. Your playing small does not serve the world. There is nothing enlightened about shrinking so that other people won't feel insecure around you. —Marianne Williamson

Works Cited

"I don't hate Lady Gaga." *US Magazine,* May 17, 2010, www.usmagazine.com.

"States of Union" *Brothers and Sisters (*Season 2) October 21, 2007.

"Male vs. Female Infant Mortality Rate Worldwide 2009." www.globalhealthfacts.org, 2009.

Abelar, Taisha. *The Sorcerer's Crossing.* New York: Penguin, 1992.

Alinsky, Saul D. *Rules for Radicals: A Pragmatic Primer for Realistic Radicals.* New York: Vintage Books, 1971.

Aristotle. *On the Generation of Animals.* Whitefish, MT: Kessinger Publishing, 2004.

Beauvoir, Simone. *The Second Sex.* New York: Vintage Press, 1989.

Brizendine, Louann. *The Female Brain.* New York: Morgan Road Books, 2006.

Campbell, Joseph, ed. *The Portable Jung.* New York: Viking Penguin, 1971.

Chadwick, David. *Crooked Cucumber: The Life and Zen Teachings of Shunryu Suzuki.* New York: Broadway Publishing, 2000.

Cutter, Martha J. *Unruly Tongue: Identity and Voice in Women's Writings 1850-1930.* Jackson, MS: University Press of Mississippi, 2008.

Denise Hallfors, Martha Waller, Daniel Bauer, Carol Ford, Carolyn Halpern. "Which Comes First in Adolescence—Sex and Drugs or Depression?" *American Journal of Preventive Medicine,* 2005: 163-170.

Durham, M. Gigi. *The Lolita Effect.* New York: Overlook Press, 2008.

Eisler, Riane. *The Chalice and the Blade: Our History, Our Future.* New York: HarperCollins, 1987.

Erikson, Erik H. *Identity: Youth and Crisis.* New York: W. W. Norton & Co, 1968.

Freire, Paulo. *Pedagogy of the Oppressed.* New York: Continuum Publishing Company, 1993.

Friedan, Betty. *The Feminine Mystique.* New York: W. W. Norton & Co, 1997.

Gilman, Charlotte Perkins. *The Yellow Wallpaper, Herland, and Selected Writings.* New York: Penguin Classics, 1999.

Gimbutas, Marija. *The Gods and Goddesses of Old Europe: Myths and Cult Images.* Berkeley, CA: University of California, 1982.

George, Kimberly B. and Letha Dawson Scanzoni. *Evangelical and Ecumenical Women's Caucus.* July 30, 2008. http://www.eewc.com (accessed March 2010).

Josselson, Ruthellen. *Finding Herself: Pathways to Identity Development in Women.* San Francisco, CA: Jossey-Bass, Inc., 1992.

Kilbourne, Jean. *Can't Buy My Love: How Advertising Changes the Way We Think and Feel.* New York: Free Press, 2000.

Labor, U S Department of. "Title IX Education Amendments of *1972.*" July 5, 2010. www.dol.gov/oasam/regs/statues/titleix.htm (accessed April 2010).

Levy, Ariel. "Dispatches from Girls Gone Wild 'Spanking on the Beach.'" *Slate.* March 24, 2004. http://www.slate.com.

—. *Female Chauvinist Pigs: Women and the Rise of the Raunch Culture.* New York: Free Press, 2005.

Lorde, Audre. "Transformation of Silence into Language and Action." In *Sister Outsider: Essay and Speeches of Audre Lorde*, by Audre Lorde. New York: Crossing Press, 2007.

McKenna, Elisabeth Perle. *When Work Doesn't Work Anymore.* New York: Dell Publishing, 1997.

Merriam-Webster's Collegiate Dictionary Tenth Edition. Springfield, MA: Merriam Webster, Inc, 2001.

Meyers, Kate. "Her Pals' Qs." *In Style*, March 2009: 304.

Morsink, Johannes. "Was Aristotle's Biology Sexist?" Vol. 12. *Journal of the History of Biology*, 1979.

Myers, Dee Dee. *Why Women Should Rule the World.* New York: Harper, 2008.

Norwood, Robin. *Women Who Love Too Much: When you keep wishing and hoping he'll change.* New York: Gallery, 2008.

Papadakis, Alison Rebecca Prince, Neil Jones, Timothy Strauman. "Self-regulation, rumination, and vulnerability to depression in adolescent girls." *Development and Psychopathology*, 2006: 815-829.

Pediatrics, American Academy of. *Caring for your School-Age Child, Ages 5 to 12.* New York: Bantam, 1999.

Pipher, Mary PhD. *Reviving Ophelia: Saving the Selves of Adolescent Girls.* New York: Ballantine Books, 1994.

Quinn, Daniel. *Ishmael: An Adventure of the Mind and Spirit.* New York: Ballantine Books, 1992.

Ravindra, Ravi. *Heart without Measure: Work with Madame de Salzmann.* Halifax, Nova Scotia: Shalia Press, 1999.

Roosevelt, Eleanor. *The Autobiography of Eleanor Roosevelt.* Cambridge, MA: Da Capoe Press, 2000.

Rosin, Hanna. "The Case Against Breastfeeding." *Atlantic Monthly*, April 2009: 64-70.

Ruiz, Don Miguel. *The Four Agreements.* San Rafael, CA: Amber-allen Publishing, 1997.

Sferrazza, Carl. *First Ladies: The Saga of President's Wives and Their Power 1789-1961.* New York: HarperPerennial, 1992.

Sprinkle, Patricia. *Women Who Do Too Much.* Grand Rapids, MI: Zondervan, 2002.

Steinem, Gloria, interview by Marianne Schnall. "Conversation with Gloria Steinem." (December 5, 2005) Feminist.com

Stepp, Laura Sessions. *Unhooked: How Young Women Pursue Sex, Delay Love and Lose at Both.* New York: Riverhead, 2007.

Suzuki, Shunryu. *Zen Mind, Beginner's Mind.* New York: Random House, 1972.

Synnott-D'Annibale, Amy. "Beauty Talk Halle Berry." *In Style*, March 2009: 209.

Tannen, Deborah. *You Just Don't Understand: Women and Men in Conversation.* New York: Harper Paperback, 2001.

Tots and Tiaras "Universal Royalty Pagent," The Discovery Channel, 2009.

Why Did I Get Married? Directed by Tyler Perry. Performed by Janet Jackson, Sharon Leal, Malik Yoba, and Tyler Perry, 2008.

Vaughn, Peggy. *The Monogamy Myth.* New York: HarperCollins, 1991.

Warner, Judith. *Perfect Madness: Motherhood in the Age of Anxiety.* New York: Riverhead Books, 2005.

West, Diana. *The Death of the Grown-Up: How America's Arrested Development is Bringing Down Western Civilization.* New York: St. Martin's Press, 2007.

Wolf, Naomi. *Fire with Fire: The New Female Power and How To Use It.* New York: Ballatine Books, 1994.

—. *The Beauty Myth: How Images of Beauty Are Used Against Women.* New York: Harper Perennial, 2002.

www.ingramcontent.com/pod-product-compliance
Ingram Content Group UK Ltd.
Pitfield, Milton Keynes, MK11 3LW, UK
UKHW041957230426
12048UKWH00008B/391